PROGRAMMING PROVERBS

Hayden Computer Programming Series

James N. Haag, Consulting Editor
Professor of Computer Science and Physics
University of San Francisco

COMPREHENSIVE STANDARD FORTRAN PROGRAMMING
James N. Haag

COMPREHENSIVE FORTRAN PROGRAMMING
James N. Haag

BASICS OF DIGITAL COMPUTER PROGRAMMING (Rev. 2nd Ed.)
John S. Murphy

BASIC BASIC: An Introduction to Computer Programming in BASIC Language
James S. Coan

DISCOVERING BASIC: A Problem Solving Approach
Robert E. Smith

BEGINNING FORTRAN: Simplified, 12-Statement Programming
John Maniotes, Harry B. Higley, and James N. Haag

ASSEMBLY LANGUAGE BASICS: An Annotated Program Book
Irving A. Dodes

PROGRAMMING PROVERBS
Henry F. Ledgard

PROGRAMMING PROVERBS FOR FORTRAN PROGRAMMERS
Henry F. Ledgard

SNOBOL: An Introduction to Programming
Peter R. Newsted

FORTRAN FUNDAMENTALS: A Short Course
Jack Steingraber

PROGRAMMING
PROVERBS

HENRY F. LEDGARD

HAYDEN BOOK COMPANY, INC.
Rochelle Park, New Jersey

ACKNOWLEDGMENTS

To Michael Flynn, my constant advisor at Johns Hopkins

To Rao Kosaraju, whose friendship, intellect, and lightheartedness have been a source of delight

To Will Fastie, who conscientiously devoted his imaginative talents towards writing the original draft of this work, and whose ready wit and energy lightened the task

To Leslie Chaikin, whose hard work added significantly to the substance of each chapter

To Joseph Davidson, who admirably served as a consultant on some of the deeper issues and who created some of the less forgotten lines

To Lee Hoevel and Ian Smith, who contributed to a sound analysis of the issues in programming

To members of the Institute for Computer Science at the National Bureau of Standards, who helped provide a solid intellectual environment for this work

To students, faculty, and secretaries in the Computer and Information Science department at the University of Massachusetts.

Library of Congress Cataloging in Publication Data

Ledgard, Henry F
 Programming proverbs.

 (Hayden computer programming series)
 Bibliography: p.
 Includes index.
 1. Electronic digital computers--Programming.
I. Title.
QA76.6.L368   001.6'424   74-22058
ISBN 0-8104-5522-6

4	5	6	7	8	9	PRINTING

77	78	79	80	81	82	YEAR

FOREWORD

By necessity, computer science, computer education, and computer practice are all embryonic human activities, for these subjects have existed for only a single generation. From the very beginning of computer activities, programming has been a frustrating black art. Individual abilities range from the excellent to the ridiculous and often exhibit very little in the way of systematic mental procedure. In a sense, the teaching of programming through mistakes and debugging can hardly be regarded as legitimate university level course work. At the university level we teach such topics as the notion of an algorithm, concepts in programming languages, compiler design, operating systems, information storage and retrieval, artificial intelligence, and numerical computation; but in order to implement ideas in any of these functional activities, we need to write programs in a specific language. Students and professionals alike tend to be over-optimistic about their ability to write programs or to make programs work according to pre-established design goals.

However, we are beginning to see a breakthrough in programming as a mental process. This breakthrough is based more on considerations of style than on detail. It involves taking style seriously, not only in how programs look when they are completed, but in the very mental processes that create them. In programming, it is not enough to be inventive and ingenious. One also needs to be disciplined and controlled in order not to become entangled in one's own complexities.

In any new area of human activity, it is difficult to foresee latent human capabilities. We have many examples of such capabilities: touch typing, speed writing, and 70-year-old grandmothers who drive down our highways at 70 miles an hour. Back in 1900 it was possible to foresee cars going 70 miles an hour, but the drivers were imagined as daredevils rather than as grandmothers. The moral is that in any new human activity, one generation hardly scratches the surface of its capabilities. So it will be in programming as well.

The next generation of programmers will be much more competent than the first one. They will have to be. Just as it was easier to get into college in the "good old days," it was also easier to get by as a programmer in the "good old days." For this new generation, a programmer will need to be capable of a level of precision and productivity never dreamed of in years gone by.

The new generation of programmers will need to acquire discipline and control, mainly by learning to write programs correctly from the start. The debugging process will take the new form of verifying that no errors are present, rather than the old form of finding and fixing errors over and over (otherwise known as "acquiring confidence by exhaustion"). Programming is a serious logical business that requires concentration and precision. In this discipline, concentration is highly related to confidence.

In simple illustration, consider a child who knows how to play a perfect game of tic-tac-toe but does not know that he knows. If you ask him to play for something important, like a candy bar, he will say to himself, "I hope I can win." And sometimes he will win, and sometimes not. The only reason he does not always win is that he drops his concentration. He does not realize this fact because he regards winning as a chance event. Consider how different the situation is when the child *knows* that he knows how to play a perfect game of tic-tac-toe. Now he does not say, "I hope I can win"; he says instead, "I know I can win; it's up to me!" And he recognizes the necessity for concentration in order to insure that he wins.

In programming as in tic-tac-toe, it is characteristic that concentration goes hand-in-hand with justified confidence in one's own ability. It is not enough simply to know how to write programs correctly. The programmer must *know that he knows* how to write programs correctly, and then supply the concentration to match.

This book of proverbs is well suited to getting members of the next generation off to the right start. The elements of style discussed here can help provide the mental discipline to master programming complexity. In essence, the book can help to provide the programmer with a large first step on the road to a new generation of programming.

Harlan D. Mills

Federal Systems Division, IBM
Gaithersburg, Md.

PREFACE

Several years ago I purchased a small book called *Elements of Style* written by William Strunk, Jr. and revised by E. B. White. Originally conceived in 1918, this book is a manual on English style. It is noted for its brevity, rigor, and deeply rooted faith in concise, clear English prose. I have read this manual several times. Each time I am again challenged to write better prose. In part, that small book is the motivation for this work.

When I began teaching courses on programming languages, I was struck by the tremendous need for style and quality in student programs. Reminded of Strunk's little book, I became concerned with the need to motivate an interest in program quality. I believe that introductory programming courses should be intimately and overtly concerned with elements of style in computer programming. This concern was brought to fruition in the summer of 1972, when the basic draft of this book was written. It was meant as a brief for people who write computer programs and who want to write them well.

Recently, there has been an increasing concern within the computing community about the quality of software. As a result, a new methodology is emerging, a harbinger of further changes to come. The ideas presented in this book depend heavily on the work of many competent researchers. Notable are the works of Dijkstra, Mills, Strachey, Hoare, Wirth, Weinberg, Floyd, Knuth, Wulf, and many others.

Several qualities other than academic ones have been deliberately sought for in this book. First, there has been an attempt to be lighthearted. It is primarily through a zest for learning that we do our best work and find it most rewarding. Second, there has been the goal of being specific. The book is written primarily in the imperative mood, and there are many examples.

This book is designed as a guide to better programming, not as an introduction to programming. As such, it should be of value to programmers who have some familiarity with programming but no great proficiency. The book may thus be used as a supplementary text in undergraduate courses where programming is a major concern. It should also be of value to experienced programmers who are seeking an informal guide to the area of quality programming. As an offshoot of its aims, I hope that programmers will begin to read and analyze programs written by others and try to reduce the intellectual effort required to read and understand their own. It is the responsibility of the programmer to program in a systematic way so that his or her work can be shared and utilized by others.

It is difficult to convey the feelings that lie behind the ideas presented here. Many programmers have told me of programming experiences in which a simple set of guidelines could have averted disaster. Although a burned hand may teach a good lesson, this book is dedicated to the proposition that there is an easier (and less painful) way to learn good programming. While I attempt to lay down guidelines for good programming, I in no way mean to remove opportunities for creativity. Rather, I hope to enable the programmer to focus that creativity on the deeper issues in programming, rather than on problems that obscure the issues.

The most difficult problem in writing this book was choosing a suitable language in which to demonstrate the principles. It seemed impossible to choose an existing language and yet maintain the objective that the book be a guide for programmers regardless of the language they use. I considered the languages BASIC, FORTRAN, COBOL, ALGOL 60, and PL/I of special importance. At first, I attempted to abstract a small "inter-lingua" or "pseudo-language" that would combine critical language constructs common to many languages. This effort met with the serious problem of introducing yet another language to the growing profusion of existing languages. Since ALGOL 60 has long been used as a communication language, it was finally adopted for this work. Since PL/I is a practical language with some closeness to ALGOL 60, a small portion of it was also adopted.

For the most part, the programming examples in the text are given in *both* ALGOL 60 and PL/I. Two basic exceptions occur. In cases where ALGOL 60 and PL/I are almost identical—for example, in arithmetic assignment statements—only one of the languages is used. In cases where generality or emphasis might be achieved by the use of other languages, examples have been given in one of these (mainly in FORTRAN and BASIC). In almost all cases, the point of the examples should be clear without a detailed knowledge of the language used.

Finally, I must admit that this book is my own personal statement about the art of programming. I am committed to the thesis that the study of principles of good programming can be of great value to all programmers and that these principles transcend the language used by any individual practitioner.

Henry F. Ledgard

CONTENTS

Chapter 1 Introduction 1

Chapter 2 Programming Proverbs 3

Proverb 1 Define the Problem Completely 5

Proverb 2 Think First, Program Later 10

Proverb 3 Use the Top-Down Approach 11

Proverb 4 Beware of Other Approaches 13

Proverb 5 Construct the Program in
Logical Units 16

Proverb 6 Use Procedures 16

Proverb 7 Avoid Unnecessary GOTO'S 19

Proverb 8 Avoid Side Effects 24

Proverb 9 Get the Syntax Correct Now,
Not Later 26

Proberb 10 Use Good Mnemonic Names 27

Proverb 11 Use Intermediate Variables Properly 29

Proverb 12 Leave Loop Variables Alone 31

Proverb 13 Do Not Recompute Constants
within a Loop 32

Proverb 14 Avoid Implementation-Dependent
Features 33

Proverb 15 Avoid Tricks 35

Proverb 16 Build in Debugging Techniques 36

Proverb 17 Never Assume the Computer
Assumes Anything 38

Proverb 18 Use Comments 40

Proverb 19 Prettyprint 42

Proverb 20 Provide Good Documentation 43

Proverb 21 Hand-Check the Program before
            Running It 44
Proverb 22 Get the Program Correct before Trying
            to Produce Good Output 48
Proverb 23 When the Program Is Correct,
            Produce Good Output 48
Proverb 24 Reread the Manual 48
Proverb 25 Consider Another Language 50
Proverb 26 Don't Be Afraid to Start Over 51
Exercises 51

Chapter 3 Top-Down Programming 64
            A Payroll Problem 67
            Kriegspiel Checkers 77
            Exercises 92

Chapter 4 Miscellaneous Topics 95
            Use of Mnemonic Names 95
            Prettyprinting 98
            Representation of Algorithms and
               Tricky Programming 102
            Procedures, Functions, and Subroutines 108
            Recursion 116
            Debugging Techniques 121
            Some Parting Comments 125
            Exercises 128

Bibliography 131
Index 133

CHAPTER ONE

INTRODUCTION

"The purpose of this here book is to learn programmers, especially them who don't want to pick up no more bad habits, to program good, easy, the first time right, and so somebody else can figger out what they done and why!"

For those readers who appreciate diamonds in the rough, the paragraph above represents this introduction as originally conceived. The following pages merely display the same diamonds cut, polished, and in a fancier setting.

An indication of the current state of the art of computer programming is the proud exclamation, "It worked the first time!" That this statement is conceivable but rarely heard indicates one prime fact: writing programs that work correctly the first time is *possible* but *unusual*. Since programmers undoubtedly try to write programs that work the first time, the question arises, "If it is possible, why is it unusual?" The answer to this question is twofold: First, programming is difficult, and second, there are very few standard methods for developing and writing good programs. Since few standard methods exist, each programmer must develop personal methods, often haphazardly. The success of these ad hoc methods depends on how well-suited they are to the problem at hand. For this reason the quality of programs varies not only between programmers, but also between programs written by the same programmer.

In reality, the state-of-the-art is considerably worse than is implied by the fact that most computer programs do not work right the first time. While there are many programs that never work at all, many more work only most of the time. More importantly, of those that work correctly, many are difficult to understand, change, or maintain.

This book is predicated on the thesis that programming is entering a new and exciting era and that programmers can and should write programs that work correctly the *first* time. For those who are accustomed to hours, days, or even

1

weeks of debugging time, this goal might seem idealistic. However, I am committed to the idea that well-founded principles can be invaluable in achieving it. Many important programming techniques are seldom obvious, even to experienced programmers. Yet with a fresh approach, many programmers may be surprised at the improvement in their ability to write correct, readable, well-structured programs.

This book is also predicated on the thesis that the ideas presented here should go *hand-in-hand* with learning any new computer language. The reader who dismisses the overall objective of this book with the comment, "I've got to learn all about my language first" may be surprised to find that the study of good programming practices along with the basics of the language may reap quick and long-standing rewards.

This book is organized in three major parts. Chapter 2 is a collection of simple rules, called *proverbs*. The proverbs summarize in terse form the major ideas of this book. Each proverb is explained and applied. A few references to later chapters are made where various ideas are more fully explored.

Chapter 3 is an introduction to a strict top-down approach for programming problems in any programming language. The approach is oriented toward the writing of correct, modular programs. It should be read carefully, because some of its details are critical and not necessarily intuitive. The approach, clearly related to an approach called "Stepwise Refinement" (see Reference W4 in the Bibliography) and an approach called "Structured Programming" (Ref. D1), hinges on developing the overall logical structure of the program first. Specific decisions, such as data representation, intermediate variables, and the like, are delayed as long as possible in order to achieve maximum flexibility.

Chapter 4 elaborates on several techniques discussed in the chapter on programming proverbs and contains a section on recursion as well. The use of these techniques should make programs easier to read and understand. They should also expedite error detection and program modifications should they become needed.

ALGOL 60 (see Reference N1 in the Bibliography) and PL/I (Ref. Z3) are used throughout the text, sometimes almost repetitiously. In a few ALGOL 60 programs, some simple, free-format input/output statements have been added to the strict ALGOL 60 language.

The reader may observe the absence of flowcharts in this book. This omission is deliberate. In the author's opinion, the use of flowcharting techniques as a method of program development has been overestimated, mainly because flowcharts can readily lead to an undue preoccupation with flow of control. The objective here is to emphasize numerous other programming techniques that have little need for flowcharts, but it must be admitted that the judicious use of flowcharts can be a valuable part of the programmer's repertoire.

CHAPTER TWO
PROGRAMMING PROVERBS

"Experience keeps a dear school, but fools will learn in no other"
Maxim prefixed to *Poor Richard's Almanack*, 1757

Over two centuries ago Ben Franklin published his now familiar *Poor Richard's Almanack*. In it he collected a number of maxims, meant as a guide for everyday living. Analogously, this chapter is intended as a simple guide to everyday programming. As such, it contains a collection of terse statements that are designed to serve as a set of practical rules for the programmer. In essence, the programming proverbs motivate the entire book.

As with most maxims or proverbs, the rules are not absolute, but neither are they arbitrary. Behind each one lies a generous nip of thought and experience. I hope the programmer will seriously consider them all. At first glance some of them may seem either trivial or too time-consuming to follow. However, I believe that experience will prove the point. Just take a look at past errors and then reconsider the proverbs.

Before going on, a prefatory proverb seems appropriate.

"Do Not Break the Rules before Learning Them"

By their nature, the programming proverbs, like all old saws, overlook much important detail in favor of an easily remembered phrase. There are some cases where programs should not conform to standard rules, that is, there are *exceptions* to every proverb. Nevertheless, I think experience will show that a programmer should not violate the rules without careful consideration of the alternatives.

A list of all the proverbs is given in Table 2.1. It is hard to weigh their relative importance, but they do at least fall into certain categories. The relative importance of one over another depends quite markedly on the programming problem at hand.

3

Table 2.1   The Programming Proverbs

Approach to the Program

1. DEFINE THE PROBLEM COMPLETELY
2. THINK FIRST, PROGRAM LATER
3. USE THE TOP-DOWN APPROACH
4. BEWARE OF OTHER APPROACHES

Coding the Program

5. CONSTRUCT THE PROGRAM IN LOGICAL UNITS
6. USE PROCEDURES
7. AVOID UNNECESSARY GOTO'S
8. AVOID SIDE EFFECTS

9. GET THE SYNTAX CORRECT NOW, NOT LATER
10. USE GOOD MNEMONIC NAMES
11. USE INTERMEDIATE VARIABLES PROPERLY
12. LEAVE LOOP VARIABLES ALONE
13. DO NOT RECOMPUTE CONSTANTS WITHIN A LOOP

14. AVOID IMPLEMENTATION-DEPENDENT FEATURES
15. AVOID TRICKS
16. BUILD IN DEBUGGING TECHNIQUES
17. NEVER ASSUME THE COMPUTER ASSUMES ANYTHING

18. USE COMMENTS
19. PRETTYPRINT
20. PROVIDE GOOD DOCUMENTATION

Running the Program

21. HAND-CHECK THE PROGRAM BEFORE RUNNING IT
22. GET THE PROGRAM CORRECT BEFORE TRYING TO PRODUCE GOOD OUTPUT
23. WHEN THE PROGRAM IS CORRECT, PRODUCE GOOD OUTPUT

In General

24. REREAD THE MANUAL
25. CONSIDER ANOTHER LANGUAGE
26. DON'T BE AFRAID TO START OVER

I must not close this introduction to the proverbs without noting why we use the word, *proverb,* rather than the more accurate word, *maxim.* Proverbs and maxims both refer to short pithy sayings derived from practical experience. Proverbs, however, are usually well-known, whereas maxims are usually not. Admittedly, the programming proverbs are not popular sayings. However, the title was chosen with an eye to the future, when hopefully some of these sayings might become true programming proverbs. And, of course, I think that "Programming Proverbs" just sounds better!

Proverb 1   DEFINE THE PROBLEM COMPLETELY

At first glance, this proverb seems so obvious as to be worthless. As the saying goes, "It's as plain as the nose on your face." True enough, but there is a tendency to take your nose for granted. Similarly, there is a tendency to assume that a problem is well defined without really examining the definition. As a result, all too often programmers begin work before they have an *exact* specification of the problem.

Consider Example 2.1, which is stated in plain English. The statements here range from the somewhat vague definition given in 2.1a, which even an experienced cook would deem ambiguous, to that of 2.1d, which is so completely specified that even the average cook should be able to follow it easily. Statement 2.1d even specifies 350°F, as opposed to 350°. Who knows, someone just might have a centigrade oven.

Example 2.1   Successively Better Problem Definitions

Statement 2.1a	Cook the chicken.
Statement 2.1b	Roast the chicken.
Statement 2.1c	Roast the chicken in a 350° oven until done.
Statement 2.1d	Roast the chicken in an oven at 350°F. Roasting times should be about 30 minutes per pound according to the following timetable:

Weight	Time
2 lb	1 hr
2-3 lb	1-1½ hr
3-4 lb	1½-2 hr
4-5 lb	2-2½ hr

More typically, consider the following simple program specification:

"Write a program that reads in a list of nonzero integers and outputs their mean."

At first glance, this specification sounds complete. On closer analysis, there prove to be a number of vague points.

(1) How long is the list? If the length of the list is to be read in explicitly, will the length be the first integer, or is the list terminated by a blank line, a special symbol, or the number zero?

(2) What is the formula for the mean and what is to be printed if the list is empty?

(3) Is the input free format or fixed format? If fixed format, what is it?

(4) What is the output to be? A message along with the mean? To how many decimal places should the mean be computed?

In the real world, programmers are often given some latitude in the final input/output characteristics of a program. Since all languages have rigid rules for the execution of programs, programmers must be specific to the last detail. In general, if something is left unspecified in the original definition, the programmer will eventually have to face the consequences. Changes made while writing the program can be annoying and distracting. In addition, some of the code already written may have to be scrapped due to oversights in the original problem definition. As a result, any critical omitted information should be defined by the programmer *before* programming.

Consider next the definition of Example 2.2a. Certain questions remain unanswered, for example, the form of the input data, the form of the check stub, and the formulas for calculating the gross and net pay. More importantly, the problem is partly defined by a specific *algorithm* stating the order of the calculations. This kind of definition should be avoided unless the implementation of a specific algorithm is actually part of the problem. The specification of an *unnecessary* algorithm clouds a program specification and restricts the class of possible solutions. A better definition is given in Example 2.2b.

Example 2.2   Proposed Definitions of a Payroll Problem

2.2a   Poor Problem Definition

    Read an employee data card.
    Calculate gross pay.
    Calculate net pay by deducting
        4% taxes and 1.75% for social security
    Print a payroll stub for the employee
    If there are more cards,
        then go back and repeat the process,
        otherwise exit the program.

2.2b   Better Problem Definition

   Input: A sequence of employee data cards with the following data:

Columns	Meaning	Format
1-5	RATE of pay per hour	dd.dd
11-15	HOURS worked per week	dd.dd

   Output: A payroll stub for each employee, printed according to the
      following format:

line 3 →	PAYROLL STUB		
line 12 →	RATE	HOURS	GROSS	NET
line 14 →	dd.dd	dd.dd	ddd.dd	ddd.dd

↑	↑	↑	↑
col 5	col 20	col 35	col 50
Rate of	Hours	Gross	Net
pay	worked	pay	pay

NETPAY = RATE * HOURS * (1 − 0.04 − 0.0175)

   As a third example, consider the definition of Example 2.3a, which defines
a program to aid a prospective homeowner in determining the financial arrange-
ments of a mortgage loan. This definition is quite adequate, but on close analysis
certain points need to be resolved. The formula that relates the values of the
principal, interest rate, number of years, and monthly payment may not be
readily available to the programmer. The formats for the input and output are
not exactly clear, and several exceptional conditions that can arise in the
computation are not mentioned. The definition of 2.3b resolves each of the
above issues. It is a bit long, but far more precise than the definition of 2.3a.

Example 2.3   Proposed Definitions of a Mortgage Problem

Example 2.3a   Adequate Problem Definition

   We wish to devise a program to help potential home-owners consider the
finances of mortgaging a home. There are four basic factors to be considered:
the principal, the interest rate, the number of years for the mortgage, and the
monthly payment. The program must input values for any three of the above
quantities, output the fourth quantity, and also output a table indicating how
the amount of the first monthly payment of each year is divided between
principal and interest.

The input to this program is a line (or card) containing three of the above four figures:

Columns	Quantity
1–5	Principal
8–11	Interest rate
14–15	Number of years
18–22	Monthly payment

The principal and number of years are given as integers, the interest rate and monthly payments are given as fixed-point real numbers. The missing quantity is given as an integer or fixed-point zero.

The output is to be a line indicating the value of the missing quantity, and a table giving, for the first monthly payment of each year, the amount contributed to decreasing the principal and the amount paid as interest.

Example 2.3b   Better Problem Definition

(1) *Problem Outline:* We wish to devise a program to help potential home-owners consider the finances of mortgaging a home. There are four basic factors to be considered:

P   The principal amount of the mortgage
I   The yearly interest rate for the mortgage
N   The number of years for the duration of the mortgage
M   The (constant) monthly payment required to pay back the principal P over N years at the interest rate I

The above quantities are related by the equation:

$$M = \frac{P * i * (1 + i)^n}{(1+i)^n - 1}$$

where

$$i = I/12 = \text{monthly interest rate}$$
$$n = 12 * N = \text{number of monthly periods in N years}$$

Briefly, the program is to input any three of the above quantities, compute and print the fourth quantity, and also print a table specifying how the first monthly payment of each year is divided between interest and principal.

(2) *Input:* The input to this program is a line (or card) of the form

column	1	8	14	18
	↓	↓	↓	↓
	ddddd	d.dd	dd	ddd.dd
	P	I	N	M

where the d's represent decimal digits such that

    P =   the principal in dollars
    I =   the percentage interest rate computed to two decimal places
    N =   the number of years in integer form
    M =   the monthly payment in dollars and cents

The value of P, I, N, or M to be computed is given as zero. Leading zeros for any value may be replaced by blanks.

(3) *Output:* The output from the program is to consist of two parts:

    (a) The value to be computed using one of the formats:

            PRINCIPAL   = $ddddd
            INTEREST RATE   = d.dd
            NUMBER OF YEARS = dd
            MONTHLY PAYMENT = $ddd.dd

    (b) A table giving for the first monthly payment of each year the amount paid to principal and the amount paid to interest. The headings and formats for the table values are as follows:

YEAR	AMT PAID TO PRINCIPAL	AMT PAID TO INTEREST
dd	$ddd.dd	$ddd.dd

Leading zeros for any value should be replaced by blanks.

(4) *Exceptional Conditions:* If any of the input values are not of the prescribed format, or if any output value is not in the range indicated, the program is to print an appropriate message to the user.

(5) *Sample Input:*

            20000   8.00   22   0.0

(6) *Sample Output for Above Input:*

            MONTHLY PAYMENT = $154.36

YEAR	AMT PAID TO PRINCIPAL	AMT PAID TO INTEREST
1	21.03	133.33
2	22.77	131.59
.		
.		
.		
25	142.53	11.83

One important point of Example 2.3b is the inclusion of a sample of the input and output. Often a sample printout can be of great value to a computer programmer in giving a quick synopsis of the problem. In addition, a sample printout can often prevent surprises in cases where the program turns out to be quite different from the expectations of the person defining the problem. If a programmer is not given a sample of the input/output, he or she should try to provide a sample *before* programming.

Before closing this discussion, one critical point must be emphasized. In practice, a programmer is often given a somewhat vague problem description and left with decisions about input/output headings, the treatment of exceptional conditions, and other factors. In such cases, the programmer should *not* begin the program until all of these alternatives have been considered and resolved.

In summary, starting the program with a fully defined problem gives a programmer a solid head start. This is the first proverb because it should be the *first* programming consideration.

Proverb 2   THINK FIRST, PROGRAM LATER

This proverb is intimately connected with a clear definition of the problem. The essence is to start thinking about the program as soon as possible, and to start the actual programming process only when the problem has been well defined and you have chosen an overall plan of attack.

Consider the first part of the proverb: *Think* means *think—do not program!* Examine the problem carefully. Consider alternative ways to solve the problem. Consider at least two different approaches. Examine the approaches in sufficient detail to discover possible trouble spots or areas in which the solution is not transparent. A top-notch program requires a top-notch algorithm. *First* means *immediately—before programming.* Start thinking as soon as possible, while the problem is fresh in your mind and the deadline is as far away as it will ever be. It is much easier to discard poor thoughts than poor programs.

The second part of the proverb is *program later.* Give yourself time to polish the algorithm thoroughly before trying to program it. This will shorten the programming time, reduce the number of false starts, and given you ample time to weed out difficult parts.

A common violation of this proverb lies in a phenomenon that we shall call the "linear" approach. In the linear approach, a programmer receives a problem and immediately starts typing or punching the code to solve it. Such an attack quickly leads to errors and patches to cover easily made mistakes. Avoid the linear approach unless you are sure the problem is really easy.

Remember Murphy's law of programming: It always takes longer to write a program than you think. A corollary might be: The sooner you start coding your program (instead of thinking), the longer it will take to finish it.

Proverb 3   USE THE TOP-DOWN APPROACH

One major point of this book is to advocate the "top-down" approach to a programming problem The top-down approach advocated here is probably *not* like conventional methods of programming. Furthermore, the top-down approach is itself subject to several interpretations, some of which we disagree with. Top-down programming is discussed at length in Chapter 3. The following description of the top-down approach is an excerpt from that chapter:

1. *Exact Problem Definition:*
The programmer starts with an *exact* statement of the problem. It is senseless to start any program without a clear understanding of the problem.

2. *Initial Language Independence:*
The programmer initially uses expressions (often in English) that are relevant to the problem solution, even though the expressions cannot be directly transliterated into the target language. From statements that are *machine and language independent,* the programmer moves toward a final machine implementation in the target language.

3. *Design in Levels:*
The programmer designs the program in *levels.* At each level, the programmer considers alternative ways to refine some parts of the previous level. The programmer may look a level or two ahead to determine the best way to design the present level.

4. *Postponement of Details to Lower Levels:*
The programmer concentrates on critical broad issues at the initial levels and postpones details (for example, input/output headings, choice of identifiers, or data representation) until lower levels.

5. *Insuring Correctness at Each Level:*
After each level, the programmer rewrites the "program" as a *correct formal statement.* This step is critically important. The program must be debugged to insure that all arguments to unwritten procedures or sections of code are then explicit and correct. Further sections of the program should be able to be written *independently,* without later changing the specifications or the interfaces between modules. The importance of being complete and explicit at each level is by far the most misunderstood aspect of the top-down approach.

6. *Successive Refinements:*
Each level of the program is successively refined and debugged until the programmer obtains the completed program in the target language.

Consider Example 2.4, which gives the initial levels of the design of a small payroll problem presented in Chapter 3. After examining the problem in detail, the programmer makes a general statement of the program, P_0. After further consideration, he decides on the overall approach to the program and obtains the

Example 2.4   Use of the Top-Down Approach in a Payroll Problem

---

P_0

Process the Payroll Cards

P_1

Initialize for program

A: read next employee card

if no more data

then calculate and print average hours worked
     stop

else process the card and check
     update for weekly average
     go back to (A) for next employee

P_2

```
/* Initialize for program */
TAXRATE      = 0.04
SS_RATE      = 0.0175
TOTAL_HOURS  = 0.0
NOS_EMPLOYEES = 0

/* read next employee card */
A:  read CARD into (NAME, SS_NUM, WAGE, HOURS)

if no more data

    then /* calculate and print average, and stop */
             AVERAGE = TOTAL_HOURS/NOS_EMPLOYEES
             print (AVERAGE)
             stop

    else /* process the card and check */
             GROSS_PAY = WAGE*HOURS
             NET_PAY   = GROSS_PAY - GROSS_PAY*TAXRATE - GROSS_PAY*SS_RATE
             print (NAME, NET_PAY, SS_NUM) on check stub

         /* update for weekly average */
             TOTAL_HOURS  = TOTAL_HOURS + HOURS
             NOS_EMPLOYEES = NOS_EMPLOYEES + 1

         /* repeat for next employee */
             goto A
```

---

more detailed description of P_1. The programmer now takes another step and refines the statements of P_1 into the more formal description of P_2. The "program" of P_2 *explicitly* specifies the decisions made in P_1. Each level is in some sense complete, and can be *debugged* as if it had been written in an actual programming language. While these initial levels are not yet written in the particular target language, successive refinements will take care of that.

Top-down programming has two distinct advantages. First, it initially frees a programmer from the confines of a programming language and allows him to deal with more natural constructs. Second, it leads to a structured modular approach, which allows the programmer to write statements relevant to the level of detail he is seeking. The details can be specified later in separate modules. In fact, the entire goal of top-down programming is just that: to aid the programmer in writing well-structured, modular programs.

Proverb 4   BEWARE OF OTHER APPROACHES

Traditionally, programmers have used many different approaches to a program. Consider the following list:

(1)   Bottom-up approach
(2)   Inside-out or forest approach
(3)   Linear approach
(4)   Typical systems analyst approach
(5)   Imitation approach

In the "bottom-up" approach, the programmer usually writes the lower procedures first and the upper levels later. The bottom-up approach is (with some critical exceptions) the mirror image of the top-down approach. It suffers severely from requiring the programmer to make specific decisions about the program *before* the overall structure is understood.

In between the top-down and the bottom-up approaches, we have the "inside-out" or "forest" approach, which consists of starting in the middle of the program and working down and up at the same time. Roughly speaking, it goes as follows:

1. *General Idea:*
First we decide upon the general idea for programming the problem.
2. *A Rough Sketch of the Program:*
Next we write any "important" sections of the program, assuming initialization in some form. In some sections we write portions of the actual code. In doing this, the actual intent of each piece of code may change several times, so that parts of our sketch may need rewriting.

3. *Coding the First Version:*

After step 2 we write specific code for the entire program. We start with the lowest level subroutines. After an individual subroutine has been coded, we should debug it and immediately prepare a description of what it does.

4. *Rethinking and Revising:*

The result of step 3 should be close to a working program, but it may be possible to improve on it. So we continue by making several improvements until we obtain a complete working program.

I think that it is fair to say that many programmers work inside out. Usually they don't start very close to the top or bottom levels. Instead they usually start in the middle and work outwards until a program finally appears on the horizon. The approach is a poor one, for the resulting program may have to undergo many changes and patches and will seldom show a clear logical structure.

The third method, already discussed, is called the "linear" approach. Here, one immediately starts writing code as it will appear when executed: first line first, second line second, and so forth. The debit with this approach is the need to make specific decisions before their consequences have been faced. This technique may seem obviously poor, but the temptation to use it can be strong.

The fourth technique is the typical "systems analyst" approach. When used wisely, it can be an effective technique, and admittedly it has been successfully used on many large programs. I shall briefly compare it to the top-down approach, the technique which is advocated in this book. The systems analyst often starts on a large programming problem by dividing up the task on the basis of the flow of control he sees in the overall program. The flow chart picturing the flow is broken into a number of programming modules that are then farmed out to the programmers. After these have been completed, the analyst will firm up the interfaces and try to make things work right. In contrast with the top-down approach, the low-level procedures receive the attention at the expense of the overall logical structure. The resulting program modules are primarily determined by the flow of control through the program Thus the importance of flow charts with this technique.

With the top-down approach, on the other hand, the flow of control is subservient to the logical structure. There will be no really identifiable flow of control on the paper upon which the program is written. The flow of control is rather like traversing a tree. It starts at the top level, goes down one or more levels, comes back, goes into another level, and so forth. The top-down approach thus has little need for flow charting.

As a final method, consider what I call the "imitation" approach, a method superficially imitating the top-down approach. This approach is discussed in detail because many programmers think that the top-down approach is really the way they have always programmed. The claim here is that there often may be subtle but *important* differences. The imitation approach is described as follows:

1. *Thinking about the Program:*

Having been given a programming assignment, take the time to examine the problem thoroughly before starting to program. Think about the details of the program for a while, and then decide on a general approach.

2. *Deciding on Procedures:*

After having thought about the problem in detail, decide what sections will be sufficiently important to merit being made into procedures.

3. *Data Representation:*

After compiling a list of such procedures, decide on a data representation that will enable the procedures to be efficient, unless the representation is already specified.

4. *Coding of Procedures:*

At this point write each procedure. After each is completed, write down what it expects as input, what it returns as output, and what it does. The procedures are written in a hierarchical manner, the most primitive first, calling procedures second, and so forth. Doing this insures that the calling sequence is fixed before a procedure is used.

5. *Coding the Main Program:*

After all procedures have been written, write the main program. The main purpose of this program will be sequencing and interfacing the subroutines.

The imitation approach possesses some important resemblances to the top-down approach. The programmer must understand the problem thoroughly before writing code, and the actual writing of the program is postponed until after certain decisions have been made. Furthermore, the problem is broken up into logical units. However, there are important different characteristics in the two approaches.

(1) In the top-down approach, a *specific* plan of attack is developed in stages. Only the issues relevant to a given level are considered, and these issues are formulated *precisely.*

(2) In the top-down approach, data representations are delayed as *long* as possible and then they are made to fit the algorithm, rather than the other way around.

(3) Furthermore, whenever the programmer decides to use a procedure or in-line section of code, the interfaces (that is, arguments, returned values, and effects) are decided *first.* The inputs and outputs are formalized before developing the procedure, that is, the procedures are made to fit the calling routine instead of the other way around.

(4) And most importantly, at *every step* in the top-down approach the programmer must have a complete, correct "program."

The major disadvantage of the "imitation" approach is that it is more likely to produce errors, require major program modifications, or result in an unstructured program. Choosing a *partially* specified attack may require serious changes to a program. Coding lower procedures first may result in a confusing program logic if the lower procedures do not happen to fit procedures designed later. Finally, early emphasis on data representation or program details may obscure an entirely better algorithm.

In summary, think *carefully* about your programming technique. The top-down approach, which is discussed at length in Chapter 3, may provide a wise alternative.

Proverb 5   CONSTRUCT THE PROGRAM IN LOGICAL UNITS

The best programs are those that can be easily understood. The logical structure should practically jump off the page. A well-structured program is always a by-product of a carefully considered design.

A good way to test for modular structure is to draw blocks and circles around the logical units of the program. A highly modular program has a structure of distinct, nonoverlapping blocks and circles. The code contained within each block or circle represents a specific computation to be carried out. The computation should be able to stand on its own merits and be readily understood. A program that has *few* blocks and circles or many *overlapping* ones is either very short or poorly structured. An outline of the logical structure for two programs performing the same computation is given in Example 2.5.

One important and often undetected problem in writing good modular programs is the elimination of *data* connections between modules. Suppose that a module M inputs a variable X and outputs a variable Y, with no transfer of control into or out of the module. Simply satisfying this transfer of control property does not guarantee that the module can be understood only in terms of the values of X and Y. If the code in M either depends on or alters variables outside of M, then the module is not isolated from changes in other modules. This difficulty frequently occurs in modules that refer to or alter global variables (variables common to several modules) or modules that input new values from an external devise. The problem is that any external change to global variables or to the input data may cause subtle changes to the functional relationship between X and Y. The simple rule of thumb: Avoid designing modules with numerous data interconnections.

In all cases, the programmer should carefully insure that the logical units of his program can be easily isolated. Following the programming proverbs can significantly add to the desired result.

Proverb 6   USE PROCEDURES

Procedure facilities are a powerful aspect of most of today's languages. The use of procedures, the notions of "functions" versus "subroutines," and the

Example 2.5 Display of Logical Structure

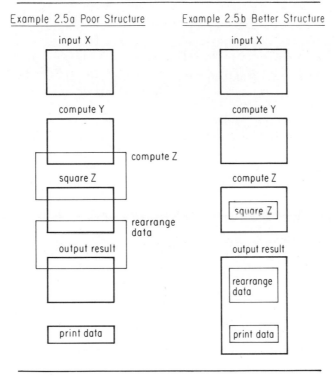

use of recursion are discussed at length in Chapter 4. We shall briefly make the case for procedures here.

Three solid reasons for using procedures are the following:

(1)   To break the program into units that expose its logical structure
(2)   To make the program more understandable
(3)   To conserve main storage needed to process a program.

Consider the programs of Example 2.6. Given the values for the three-element arrays A, B, C, and D, the program uses the determinant method (assuming DENOM is nonzero) to solve three independent equations of the form.

$$A_1 X + B_1 Y + C_1 Z = D_1$$
$$A_2 X + B_2 Y + C_2 Z = D_2$$
$$A_3 X + B_3 Y + C_3 Z = D_3$$

for the unknowns X, Y and Z.

The program of 2.6a is a confusion of arithmetic calculations. It contains little hint of the determinant method or the algorithm needed to solve the

Example 2.6   Use of Procedures

2.6a.   Poor: Solution without Using Procedures

```
DENOM := A[1]*B[2]*C[3] + A[2]*B[3]*C[1] + A[3]*B[1]*C[2]
         - A[3]*B[2]*C[1] - A[2]*B[1]*C[3] - A[1]*B[3]*C[2];

X     := D[1]*B[2]*C[3] + D[2]*B[3]*C[1] + D[3]*B[1]*C[2]
         - D[3]*B[2]*C[1] - D[2]*B[1]*C[3] - D[1]*B[3]*C[2];
Y     := A[1]*D[2]*C[3] + A[2]*D[3]*C[1] + A[3]*D[1]*C[2]
         - A[3]*D[2]*C[1] + A[2]*D[1]*C[3] - A[1]*D[3]*C[2];
Z     := A[1]*B[2]*D[3] - A[2]*B[3]*D[1] + A[3]*B[1]*D[2]
         - A[3]*B[2]*D[1] - A[2]*B[1]*D[3] - A[1]*B[3]*D[2];

X     := X/DENOM;
Y     := Y/DENOM;
Z     := Z/DENOM;
```

2.6b.   Better: Solution Using Procedures

```
procedure  DET(X1,X2,X3,Y1,Y2,Y3,Z1,Z2,Z3);
           DET := X1*Y2*Z3 + X2*Y3*Z1 + X3*Y1*Z2
                  - X3*Y2*Z1 - X2*Y1*Z3 - X1*Y3*Z2;
end DET;

DENOM := DET(A[1], B[1], C[1], A[2], B[2], C[2], A[3], B[3], C[3]);

X := DET(D[1], B[1], C[1], D[2], B[2], C[2], D[3], B[3], C[3])/DENOM;
Y := DET(A[1], D[1], C[1], A[2], D[2], C[2], A[3], D[3], C[3])/DENOM;
Z := DET(A[1], B[1], D[1], A[2], B[2], D[2], A[3], B[3], D[3])/DENOM;
```

2.6c.   Still Better: Solution Using Procedures and Passing Arrays as Arguments

```
procedure DET(R,S,T);   array R,S,T;

   DET := R[1]*S[2]*T[3] + R[2]*S[3]*T[1] + R[3]*S[1]*T[2]
          - R[3]*S[2]*T[1] - R[2]*S[1]*T[3] - R[1]*S[3]*T[2];
end DET;

DENOM := DET(A,B,C);

X     := DET(D,B,C)/DENOM;
Y     := DET(A,D,C)/DENOM;
Z     := DET(A,B,D)/DENOM;
```

---

problem. In contrast, Example 2.6b uses a procedure to calculate the determinants. It is explicitly clear that each unknown is the quotient of two determinants and that the denominator is the determinant of the variable coefficient matrix. Example 2.6c shows an even greater improvement in which the arrays as opposed to array elements are passed as arguments.

In brief, use procedures often. They can make your program shorter, more structured, and easier to understand.

Proverb 7   AVOID UNNECESSARY GOTO'S

The unconditional transfer of control, the GOTO statement, has been associated with programming since its inception. Its historical ties have left indelible marks on today's major programming languages. Until recently, virtually all higher level languages have had some form of an unrestricted GOTO. Yet, of all the linguistic constructs in today's languages, few have been debated more often or more intensively. The GOTO is not intrinsically evil, but its abuses can be avoided by using more transparent linguistic features.

Consider first Examples 2.7 and 2.8, and notice the elimination of GOTO s in favor of looping constructs, conditional statements, and built-in functions.

Example 2.7 Elimination of GOTO's in Favor of Looping Constructs

2.7a. Poor	2.7b. Better
ALGOL 60	ALGOL 60
| ```
    S := 0;
    T := 1;
L1: if I > 100 then goto L2;
    S := S + I;
    I := I + 1;
    goto L1;
L2: print (S);
``` | ```
S := 0;
for I := 1 step 1 until 100 do
    S := S + I;
print (S);
``` |
| PL/I | PL/I |
| ```
    S = 0;
    I - 1;
L1: IF I > 100 THEN GOTO L2;
    S = S + I
    I = I + 1;
    GOTO L1;
L2: PUT LIST(S);
``` | ```
S = 0;
DO I = 1 BY 1 TO 100;
    S = S + I;
END;
PUT LIST(S);
``` |

Example 2.8 Elimination of GOTO's in Favor of Conditional Statements and Built-in Functions

2.8a. Poor	2.8b. Better
| ```
    if A ≤ B then goto L2;
    D := A - B;
    goto L3;
L2: D := B - A;
L3: print (D);
``` | ```
if A > B then D := A - B
          else D := B - A;
print (D);
``` |

2.8c. Best

```
print(abs(A-B));
```

When the GOTO's are removed, a clearer structure arises, and the program length shortens.

GOTO's are often the result of "band-aids" or patches in the modification of a program. Consider the somewhat contrived BASIC programs of Example 2.9, written using a text-editor with line numbers. In his first program draft the programmer unfortunately chose to number his statements with successive even numbers. After some thought and error messages, he managed to piece together the program of Example 2.9a. Then he managed to perform the same calculations without the GOTO's, as shown in 2.9b. This program is seven lines shorter and eliminates the transfers of control. Schematic diagrams of the flow of control of these two programs are given in Figs. 2.1 and 2.2. (Note: the extrapolation from this simple program to more sophisticated programs should not be missed.)

Example 2.9   Elimination of GOTO's in BASIC program

```
2.9a.   First Program              2.9b.   Second Program

   10   LET S = 0                     10   LET S = 0
   11   GO TO 30                      20   INPUT N
   12   LET Y = S/4                   30   FOR I = 1 TO N
   14   LET J = S/3                   40       LET S = S + I
   15   GO TO 34                      50   NEXT I
   16   LET X = Y*J + X               60   LET Y = S/4
   18   PRINT S,X                     70   LET J = S/3
   20   STOP                          80   LET X = Y*J + 2*S
   22   FOR I = 1 TO N                90   PRINT   S,X
   24       LET S = S + I            100   END
   26   NEXT I
   28   GO TO 12
   30   INPUT N
   32   GO TO 22
   34   LET X = 2*S
   36   GO TO 16
   38   END
```

As an example illustrating an extreme use of GOTO's and a corresponding complete elimination of GOTO's, consider the ALGOL 60 programs of Example 2.10 and the following description of the water-jug problem:

Suppose we have two jugs, JUG5 which can hold 5 gallons of water, and JUG8 which can hold 8 gallons of water. We wish to write a program to "simulate" a random sequence of events whereby the 8 gallon jug will end up with exactly 2 gallons of water. An event consists of either (a) filling either jug with water from a tap, (b) emptying either jug down a drain, or (c) pouring one jug into the other.

The programs of Example 2.10 assume the definition of a function RANDOM that inputs two integers n_1 and n_2 and outputs a randomly selected

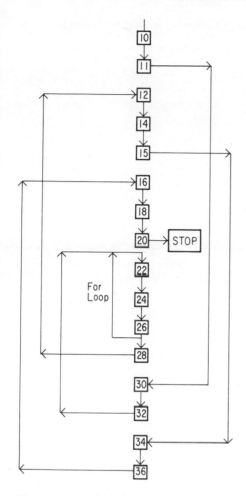

Fig. 2.1 Flow of control in patched
program

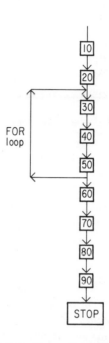

Fig. 2.2 Flow of control in completely rewritten program

Example 2.10   Solution of Water Jug Problem in ALGOL 60

2.10a With GOTO's	2.10b. Without GOTO's

```
        switch  A := L1,L2,L3,L4,L5,L6;          JUG5 := JUG8 := 0;
        JUG5 := JUG8 := 0;
                                                 do I := RANDOM(1,6) while (JUG8 ≠ 2)
                                                    if     I - 1 then JUG8 :- 0  else
LO:   I     := RANDOM(1,6);                            if I = 2 then JUG5 := 0  else
      goto A(I);                                      if I = 3 then JUG5 := 5  else
                                                      if I = 4 then JUG8 := 8  else
L1:   JUG8 := 0;                                       if I = 5 then
      goto L9;
```

Example 2.10   Solution of Water Jug Problem in ALGOL 60 (cont'd)

```
L2:   JUG5 := 0;                            begin
      goto L9;                              if (JUG5 + JUG8) > 8
L3:   JUG5 := 5;                            then begin
      goto L9;                                 JUG5 := JUG5 - (8 - JUG8);
L4:   JUG8 := 8;                               JUG8 := 8 end
      goto L9;                              else begin
L5:   if (JUG5 + JUG8) > 8                     JUG8 := JUG8 + JUG5;
          then goto L7;                        JUG5 := 0 end;
      JUG8 := JUG8 + JUG5;                  end                        else
      goto L2;                           if I = 6 then
L6:   if (JUG5 + JUG8) > 5                  begin
          then goto L8;                     if (JUG5 + JUG8) > 5
      JUG5 := JUG5 + JUG8;                  then begin
      goto L1;                                 JUG8 := JUG8 - (5 - JUG5);
L7:   JUG5 := JUG5 - (8 - JUG8);               JUG5 := 5 end
      goto L4;                              else begin
L8:   JUG8 := JUG8 - (5 - JUG5);               JUG5 := JUG5 + JUG8;
      goto L3;                                 JUG8 := 0 end;

L9:   if JUG8 ≠ 2  then goto L0;            end;

                                         print ('SOLUTION FOUND');
      print ('SOLUTION FOUND');
```

integer inclusively between n_1 and n_2. The claim here is that the GOTO-oriented program is not as transparent as its GOTO-less counterpart. The reader is invited to draw his own conclusion.

In a more typical setting, consider the programs of Example 2.11. These programs employ a variation of the bubble sort algorithm to sort an array A containing N entries. The procedure SWAP exchanges the values of the two variables given as arguments. Basically, the programs scan the array A once from left (position 1) to right (position N). At each position examined in the array, the elements to the left of the position are already in order, and the program checks to see if the element in the next position is itself in order. If not, the element is swapped with the previous element and then it is "bubbled" left until its proper place in the sorted part of the array is found. Processing then continues at the position to the right of the element originally examined.

The PL/I and ALGOL 60 programs of Example 2.11a are oriented towards an efficient use of the GOTO statement. The resulting programs are somewhat difficult to understand. The programs of Example 2.11b avoid the use of GOTO altogether.

One major point of this example is that the (possibly) small gain in efficiency via the GOTO is not as important as the improvement in clarity when the programmer uses alternative ways of constructing his program. (Note: There are two calls to the procedure SWAP; do you see how to shorten the programs so that only one call to SWAP is used?)

Example 2.11   A Variant of the Bubble Sort Algorithm

2.11a. Poor   2.11b. Better

PL/I   PL/I

```
        J = 1;                         DO J = 1 TO N-1;
                                         IF A(J) > A(J+1) THEN
A:      IF J = N THEN GOTO D;          BEGIN;
        IF A(J) <= A(J+1) THEN GOTO C;     CALL SWAP (A(J),A(J+1));
        CALL SWAP(A(J),A(J+1));            DO K = J-1 BY -1 TO 1
        K = J;                                WHILE A(K) > A(K+1);
                                              CALL SWAP(A(K),A(K+1));
B:      K = K - 1;                        END;
        IF K = 0 | A(K) <= A(K+1)       END;
            THEN GOTO C;               END;
        CALL SWAP(A(K),A(K+1));
        GOTO B;                        PUT LIST (A);

C:      J = J + 1;
        GOTO A;

D:      PUT LIST (A);
```

ALGOL 60   ALGOL 60

```
        J := 1;                       for J := 1 step 1 until N-1 do
                                          if A[J] > A[J+1] then
A:      if J = N then goto D;                begin SWAP(A[J],A[J+1]);
        if A[J] < A[J+1] then goto C;              K := J;
        SWAP(A[J],A[J+1]);                         for K := K-1 while K > 1 ∧
        K := J;                                        A[K] > A[K+1]
                                                   do SWAP(A[K],A[K+1]);
B:      K := K - 1;                          end;
        if K = 0 ∨ A[K] < A[K+1]
            then goto C;              print (A);
        SWAP(A[K],A[K+1]);
        goto B;

C:      J := J + 1;
        goto A;

D:      print (A);
```

In summary, the deeper issue here is not merely the elimination of GOTO's but the use of a clear, logical program structure. A programmer would be well advised to try an alternative approach when a GOTO is required. Generally speaking, GOTO's can be used wisely, but they can often be abused. The problem with GOTO's is that when they are abused, they can lead a programmer (and his successors) down the path of a confusing, almost spaghetti-like logic. If a logical program structure is achieved, then GOTO's will have found their proper place.

Proverb 8   AVOID SIDE EFFECTS

An "effect" occurs in a procedure if anything is changed that is external to the procedure. If this effect is not the main purpose of the procedure, it is known as a "side effect." Side effects may cause subtle errors that are extremely hard to track down. The most common source of side effects is the alteration of global variables, that is, variables that are known throughout the program.

Consider the problem of a polynomial approximation to the sine function. The sine of a number X can be approximated by the following trigonometric series:

$$\text{sine } X = X - \frac{X^3}{3!} + \frac{X^5}{5!} - \frac{X^7}{7!} + \ldots$$

We wish to test this computation to see how fast this series converges to a known value of SINE(X). Since we know that SINE($\pi/2$) = 1, we can write the following codes for the main routine:

PL/I

```
PI = 3.14159265;
DO ORDER = 1 BY 2 TO 15;
      ANSWER = APPROX(PI/2,ORDER);
      PUT LIST(ORDER, ANSWER);
END;
```

ALGOL 60

```
PI := 3.14159265;
for ORDER := 1 step 1 until 15 do
      begin ANSWER := APPROX(PI/2,ORDER);
            print(ORDER, ANSWER)
end;
```

This sequence invokes the procedure APPROX several times, and after each invocation, the order of the highest order term in the approximation is incremented. For example, when ORDER is 5, the sine of X is approximated by

$$X - \frac{X^3}{3!} + \frac{X^5}{5!}$$

To perform this test we must devise the procedure APPROX. Consider the two procedures defined in Examples 2.12a and b. Checked *individually* with the main routine declarations,

PL/I	*ALGOL 60*

DECLARE (SIGN,N,PRODUCT) FIGXED; → DECLARE (SIGN,N,PRODUCT) FIXED;
integer SIGN,N,PRODUCT;
DECLARE SUM FLOAT;
real SUM;

both functions perform correctly. However, when the procedures in Example 2.12 are run *together* with the main routine, the program loops indefinitely. The reader may wonder how such errors arise. (*Try to find the bug before reading the rest of this section.*) A program is usually coded in several parts, and the programmer may not be careful to check whether the variables he is using represent distinct quantities. In particular, the problem in Example 2.12a is that the two functions interact. The global variable N is used as the loop variable for both procedures, and whenever the FACT procedure is called, the loop variable N in APPROX is reset to 1. The series thus obtained for the sine of X is

$$X - \frac{X^3}{3!} + \frac{X^3}{3!} - \frac{X^3}{3!} + \dots$$

In Example 2.12b N is declared *local* to each function, along with the rest of the internally used variables. The convergence test performs as expected.

Many languages, such as BASIC and COBOL, do not have facilities for declaring local variables. Nevertheless, the concept may still be applied.

Example 2.12 Procedures for Polynomial Approximation to the Sine Function

2.12a   Incorrect Procedures

```
       PL/I                                    ALGOL 60

APPROX: PROCEDURE(X,ORDER)              real procedure APPROX(X,ORDER);
        RETURNS(FLOAT);                 real X; integer ORDER;
DECLARE X FLOAT, ORDER FIXED;           begin
    SUM = 0;                                SUM := 0;
    SIGN = +1;                              SIGN := +1;
    DO N = 1 BY 2 TO ORDER;                 for N := 1 step 2 until ORDER do
       SUM = SUM +                          begin
           SIGN*(X**N)/FACT(N);                SUM := SUM + SIGN*(X↑N)/FACT(N);
       SIGN = - SIGN;                          SIGN := -SIGN;
    END;                                    end;
    RETURN (SUM);                           APPROX := SUM;
END APPROX;                             end APPROX;

FACT:  PROCEDURE(NUMBER)                integer procedure FACT(NUMBER);
       RETURNS(FIXED);                  integer NUMBER;
DECLARE NUMBER FIXED;                   begin
    PRODUCT = 1;                            PRODUCT := 1;
    DO N = NUMBER BY -1 TO 1;               for N := NUMBER step -1 until 1
        PRODUCT = N*PRODUCT;                do  PRODUCT := N*PRODUCT;
    END;                                    FACT := PRODUCT;
    RETURN (PRODUCT);                   end FACT;
END FACT;
```

Example 2.12   Procedures for Polynomial Approximation to the Sine Function (cont'd)

2.12b   Correct Procedures

PL/I	ALGOL 60

```
APPROX:  PROCEDURE(X,ORDER)
            RETURNS(FLOAT);
         DECLARE (ORDER,SIGN,N) FIXED;
         DECLARE (X,SUM) FLOAT;
            SUM  = 0;
            SIGN = +1;
            DO N = 1 BY 2 TO ORDER;
               SUM  = SUM +
                    SIGN*(X**N)/FACT(N);
               SIGN = -SIGN ;
            END;
            RETURN (SUM);
         END APPROX;


   FACT:  PROCEDURE(NUMBER)
            RETURNS(FIXED);
         DECLARE (PRODUCT,NUMBER,N) FIXED;
            PRODUCT = 1;
            DO N = NUMBER BY -1 TO 1;
               PRODUCT = N*PRODUCT;
            END;
            RETURN (PRODUCT);
         END FACT;
```

```
real procedure APPROX(X,ORDER);
real X; integer ORDER;
begin integer SIGN,N; real SUM;
   SUM  := 0;
   SIGN := +1;
   for N := 1 step 2 until ORDER do
      begin
      SUM  := SUM + SIGN*(X↑N)/FACT(N);
      SIGN := -SIGN;
      end;
   APPROX := SUM;
end APPROX;


integer procedure FACT(NUMBER);
integer NUMBER;
begin integer PRODUCT, N;
   PRODUCT := 1;
   for N := NUMBER step -1 until 1
   do   PRODUCT := N*PRODUCT;
   FACT := PRODUCT;
end FACT;
```

For a more extended discussion of side effects, see Chapter 4. In any case, avoid side effects. They can be a deadly source of errors.

Proverb 9   GET THE SYNTAX CORRECT NOW, NOT LATER

How many times have you heard a compiler being roundly cursed for not accepting a missing semicolon, a missing parenthesis, or some other "trivial" feature of syntax? Consider the program segments of Example 2.13. Errors like the ones in this example should have been screened in advance by a careful programmer.

There is little excuse for syntactic errors in programs, since the manual specifies the syntax for you. The time to consider syntax is *not* while debugging your completed program. Keep the manual handy as you write your code, and if you are not absolutely positive that the syntax of the statement you are writing is perfect, look it up. It only takes a few seconds, and your grasp of the language will increase with constant references to the manual.

You can and should write programs that are completely *free of syntactic errors on the* first *trial run.* I mean it. It can be done, but you first must

Example 2.13   Some Simple Syntactic Errors

		Wrong		Right

PL/I
- (1) A = B↑C + D;   (1) A = B**C + D;
- (2) FORMAT (F(7.3));   (2) FORMAT (F(7,3));
- (3) DECLARE A,B,C FIXED;   (3) DECLARE (A,B,C) FIXED;

ALGOL 60
- (1) for I = 1 step 1 until 5   (1) for I := 1 step 1 until 5
- (2) procedure P(X); integer X;   (2) procedure P(X); value X;
        value X;   integer X;
- (3) X := X + 1;   (3) X := X + 1;
    if X = Y then Z := 1;   if X = Y then Z := 1
            else Z := 2;   else Z := 2;
    Z := F(X,Y,Z);   Z := F(X,Y,Z);

FORTRAN
- (1) READ(5) (A(I)I = 1,5)   (1) READ(5) (A(I), I = 1,5)
- (2) FORMAT (F5.6)   (2) FORMAT (F6.5)
- (3) CALL SUBROUTINE F(X,Y)   (3) CALL F(X,Y)

BASIC
- (1) LET MAT A = B   (1) MAT A = B
- (2) READ MAT A   (2) MAT READ A

COBOL
- (1) 02 TO PICTURE IS A(30)   (1) 02 INDENT PICTURE IS A(30)
- (2) COMPUTE A = B*C   (2) COMPUTE A = B * C

convince yourself that you indeed can do it. If that doesn't impress you, think of all the hours of turnaround time or on-line debugging time you can waste tracking down the errors.

Proverb 10   USE GOOD MNEMONIC NAMES

It is hard to underestimate the value of using good mnemonic names. It is all too easy to become careless and use names that may later confuse the entire intent of a program. This topic is discussed in detail in Chapter 4. For the moment, it is sufficient to make one point: Use names that imply their role in the program.

The disadvantage of poor names is easily seen in Example 2.14. The programmer who writes code like that in Example 2.14a will probably need to keep a separate list specifying what each variable name represents. Otherwise he may lose track of what each variable does. Example 2.14b clarifies the situation completely. The variable names themselves state the intended calculation. Example 2.14b was purposely written using variable names with a maximum length of six characters, the requirement in standard FORTRAN. Examples 2.14c, 2.14d, and 2.14e illustrate the possibilities available in languages like PL/I, ALGOL 60,

Example 2.14   Use of Mnemonic Names

2.14a.   Poor

```
X1 = X2*X3 + X4*X5;
X6 = X7*X1;
X8 = X9*X1;
X  = X1 - X6 - X8;
```


2.14b.   Better

```
GROSS = WAGE*HOURS + OVTIM*EXHRS;
TAX   = RATE*GROSS;
SS    = SSRATE*GROSS;
NET   = GROSS - TAX - SS;
```


2.14c.   The PL/I Option

```
GROSS_PAY    = WAGE * HOURS + OVERTIME_WAGE * EXTRA_HOURS;
TAX          = TAX_RATE * GROSS_PAY;
SOC_SECURITY = SOC_SEC_RATE * GROSS_PAY;
NET_PAY      = GROSS_PAY - TAX - SOC_SECURITY;
```


2.14d.   The ALGOL 60 Option

```
GROSSPAY     := WAGE * HOURS + OVERTIMEWAGE * EXTRAHOURS;
TAX          := TAXRATE * GROSSPAY;
SOCSECURITY  := SOCSECRATE * GROSSPAY;
NETPAY       := GROSSPAY - TAX - SOCSECURITY;
```


2.14e.   The COBOL Option

```
COMPUTE GROSS-PAY ROUNDED     = WAGE * HOURS + OVERTIME-WAGE * EXTRA-HOURS.
COMPUTE TAX ROUNDED           = TAX-RATE * GROSS-PAY.
COMPUTE SOC-SECURITY ROUNDED  = SOC-SEC-RATE * GROSS-PAY.
COMPUTE NET-PAY               = GROSS-PAY - TAX - SOC-SECURITY.
```

---

and COBOL, which allow lengthy names.* OVERTIME_WAGE and OVER TIMEWAGE are certainly more informative than OVTIME.

The major reason for using good mnemonic names is to improve readability. It is worth the extra time to devise and make use of informative names. A programmer may not fully appreciate this fact until he has written a large program which he has to debug or modify months later. The mnemonic assistance is then priceless.

---

*Note for ALGOL 60 programmers: Writing "OVERTIME WAGE" instead of "OVERTIMEWAGE" is acceptable in ALGOL 60. Do you know why?

Proverb 11   USE INTERMEDIATE VARIABLES PROPERLY

In many languages, complex mathematical expressions can be written in a single line of code. For clarity it is often advantageous to split up such expressions and use intermediate variables. Consider Example 2.15. The change from 2.15a to 2.15b is quite illuminating.

Example 2.15   Use of Intermediate Variables for Clarity

2.15a.   Poor

```
RESULT = LOG(SQRT(L-2*FULL(R-Y))) + 7*FLOOR(RANDOM(3) - P1*3) + 4*FULL(Y-R);
```

2.15b.   Better

```
LOG_PART       = LOG(SQRT(L-2*FULL(R-Y)));
INTEGER_PART   = 7*FLOOR(RANDOM(3) - P1*3);
CONSTANT_PART  = 4*FULL(Y-R);
RESULT         = LOG_PART + INTEGER_PART + CONSTANT_PART;
```

Intermediate variables may also be used to make the program more efficient, as in Example 2.16. Instead of computing the discriminant,

$$B{\uparrow}2 - 4*A*C$$

in each of the three conditional clauses, it is necessary to compute the discriminant only once and store it in DISCR. Situations in which a single quantity is required for several statements within a program are common, and frequently you will be able to speed up your algorithm by computing these quantities just one time.

Example 2.16   Use of Intermediate Variables for Efficiency

2.16a.   Poor

```
if (B↑2 - 4*A*C) > 0 then print ('ROOTS ARE REAL AND UNEQUAL');
if (B↑2 - 4*A*C) = 0 then print ('ROOTS ARE REAL AND EQUAL');
if (B↑2 - 4*A*C) < 0 then print ('ROOTS ARE COMPLEX');
```

2.16b.   Better

```
DISCR := B↑2 - 4*A*C;
if DISCR > 0 then print ('ROOTS ARE REAL AND UNEQUAL');
if DISCR = 0 then print ('ROOTS ARE REAL AND EQUAL');
if DISCR < 0 then print ('ROOTS ARE COMPLEX');
```

However, beware of overkill. The use of too many intermediate variables can even be worse than what they replace. Consider Example 2.17. The use of nine variables here is quite ridiculous.

Example 2.17   Use of Too Many Intermediate Variables

2.17a. Poor	2.17b. Better
| ```
B2      = B**2;
END     = 4*A*C;
DISCR   = B2 - END;
ROOT    = SQRT(DISCR);
NUM1    = -B + ROOT;
NUM2    = -B - ROOT;
DENOM   = 2*A;
ROOT1   = NUM1/DENOM;
ROOT2   = NUM2/DENOM;
``` | ```
DISCR = B**2 - 4*A*C;
ROOT1 = (-B + SQRT(DISCR))/(2*A);
ROOT2 = (-B - SQRT(DISCR))/(2*A);
```

2.17c. Still Better

```
X     = SQRT(B**2 - 4*A*C);
ROOT1 = (-B + X)/(2*A);
ROOT2 = (-B - X)/(2*A);
``` |

As a final example, consider the recursive procedures of Example 2.18, which defines the Moibius function, F. For a given value $N \geqslant 1$,

$$F(N) \quad = \begin{cases} 1 & \text{if } N = 1 \\ 0 & \text{if a prime factor is contained in } N \text{ more than once} \\ (-1)^p & \text{if } N \text{ is the product of } p \text{ different prime factors.} \end{cases}$$

For example, $F(5) = -1$ because 5 is prime, $F(24) = 0$ because $24 = 2*2*2*3$, and $F(77) = 1$ because $77 = 7*11$.

For the construction of F, an integer function PRIME is available. If $N > 1$, PRIME (N) returns the smallest prime factor of N; if $N = 1$, PRIME(N) returns 1. In Example 2.18a no intermediate variables are used; in Example 2.18b an

Example 2.18   Use of an Intermediate Variable in the Definition of the Moibius Function

2.18a. Poor	2.18b. Better
PL/I	PL/I
| ```
F: PROCEDURE(N)  RECURSIVE
      RETURNS(FIXED);
   DECLARE N FIXED;
   IF N = 1
      THEN RETURN(1);
      ELSE IF PRIME(N/PRIME(N))
               = PRIME(N)
      THEN RETURN(0);
      ELSE RETURN(-F(N/PRIME(N)));
END;
``` | ```
F: PROCEDURE(N)  RECURSIVE
      RETURNS(FIXED);
   DECLARE (N,P1) FIXED;
   P1 = PRIME(N);
   IF N = 1
      THEN RETURN(1);
      ELSE IF PRIME(N/P1) = P1
               THEN RETURN(0);
               ELSE RETURN(-F(N/P1));
END;
``` |

ALGOL 60	ALGOL 60

```
integer procedure F(N);
integer N;
if N = 1
  then F := 1
  else if PRIME(N/PRIME(N))
          = PRIME(N)
      then F := 0
      else F := -F(N/PRIME(N))
```

```
integer procedure F(N);
integer N;
begin integer P1;
  P1 := PRIME(N);
  if N = 1
    then F := 1
    else if PRIME(N/P1) = P1
          then F := 0
          else F := -F(N/P1)
end;
```

intermediate variable P1 = PRIME(N) is used to obtain the smallest prime factor of N. The use of this intermediate variable helps clarify the somewhat confusing calculations of Example 2.18a. Furthermore, in Example 2.18b the value of PRIME(N) is computed only once.

Generally, the proper use of intermediate variables is not easy. Nevertheless, judicious use can lead to more readable and efficient programs.

Proverb 12   LEAVE LOOP VARIABLES ALONE

Taken in a certain light, loop variables should be considered constants. During the execution of a loop, neither the value of the active loop variable itself nor the values of the variables in an increment expression should be changed. In the extreme case, the updating of loop variables is easy to illustrate; it is shown in Example 2.19. This loop updates A[2] to 2*A[1] indefinitely. Naturally, it isn't really infinite. If the computer doesn't break down first, eventually A[2] will get so big that it will not fit into a single storage location and will cause an "overflow."

Example 2.19 Infinite Loop Caused by Directly Changing the Value of a Loop Variable

PL/I	ALGOL 60

```
DO I = 2 BY 1 UNTIL 10;
   I = I - 1;
   A[I+1] = 2*A[I];
END;
```

```
for I := 2 step 1 until 10 do
   begin I := I - 1;
         A[I+1] := 2*A[I]
   end;
```

Consider also Example 2.20. How many times is this loop executed? What is the value of N that will be printed? The answers in this case are almost

Example 2.20 Confusing Loop Execution Caused by Indirectly Changing the Loop Variable

PL/I	ALGOL 60
| ```
F:  PROCEDURE (M);
    M = M - 1;
    RETURN(2*M);
END F;

N = 1;
DO I = 1 BY 2 UNTIL 100;
    IF I > N THEN N = N + F(I);
              ELSE N = N - 1;
END;
PUT LIST(N);
``` | ```
integer procedure  F(M);
begin M := M - 1;
      F := 2*M;
end F;

N := 1;
for I := 1 step 2 until 100 do
    if I > N then N := N + F(I)
              else N := N - 1;
print(N);
``` |

impossible to give without a hard look at the program. In practice, the altering of loop variables can be very subtle. Consequently, any errors introduced will be just as subtle. As a general practice within a loop, *never* change the loop variable or a variable in an incrementing expression. If you do, you'll be inviting problems.

Proverb 13   DO NOT RECOMPUTE CONSTANTS WITHIN A LOOP

How do you recompute a constant? The answer to that question is easy. Just compute the constant within the body of a loop, and then it will be recomputed for each iteration. The same principle applies here as in the discussion of efficiency using intermediate variables. Do not make unnecessary computations. Take repeated calculations outside the range of the loop. While one of the major concerns of this book is to emphasize the quality, structure, and correctness of programs (perhaps even at the expense of efficiency), unnecessary computations are to be clearly avoided.

Example 2.21 shows a simple but obvious example. Take the familiar equation for the volume of a sphere:

$$V = \frac{4}{3}\pi R^3$$

Note that $(4/3)\,\pi$ is always constant, regardless of the value of R. So in 2.21a the constant is calculated 100 times, whereas in 2.21b it has been factored out and computed once.

Well, 100 multiplications aren't all that many, but suppose there were 10,000. In programs with vast amounts of data, 10,000 computations are not unusual. At $1000 per hour, which is what some computers cost, time is really money.

Example 2.21   Taking a "Constant" out of a Loop

2.21a.   Poor

PL/I

```
P1 = 3.14159;
DO R = 1 BY 1 UNTIL 100;
    V = (4*PI*(R**3))/3;
    PUT LIST (R,V);
END;
```

2.21b.   Better

PL/I

```
PI = 3.14159;
CONSTANT = 4*PI/3;
DO R = 1 BY 1 UNTIL 100;
    V = CONSTANT*(R**3);
    PUT LIST (R,V);
END;
```

ALGOL 60

```
PI := 3.14159;
for R := 1 step 1 until 100 do
    begin V := 4*PI*(R↑3)/3;
        print (R,V);
    end
```

ALGOL 60

```
PI      := 3.14159;
CONSTANT := 4*PI/3;
for R := 1 step 1 until 100 do
    begin V := CONSTANT*(R↑3);
        print (R,V);
    end
```

Proverb 14   AVOID IMPLEMENTATION-DEPENDENT FEATURES

As technology rapidly changes, computers and language processors change. In addition, programmers themselves may move to a different installation. Generally speaking, a programmer should write his programs so that changing to a different machine or language processor will not force him to rewrite his programs. To make sure of this, he should write in a subset of the reference language that avoids the frills and the implementation-dependent features, which are always the first to go when new hardware or software is introduced. A program written without implementation-dependent features will have a better chance of being "portable," that is, able to be run directly on a different language processor other than the original one.

Consider Example 2.22 in ALGOL 60. The ALGOL 60 report does *not* specify the order of evaluation of the actual parameters in an actual parameter list. In a left-to-right order of evaluation, the integer 25 is printed. In a right-to-left implementation, the integer 36 is printed.

Consider Example 2.23a in BASIC. This program works only on a machine that accepts *extended* BASIC. For example, a machine that takes an earlier or different version of BASIC may not accept the statement,

$$S = 0$$

whereas all versions will accept the statement,

$$LET\ S = 0$$

Example 2.22 An Implementation-Dependent Feature Found in ALGOL 60

```
begin
      integer A;
      integer procedure F(X);
            begin X := X + 1;
                  F := X↑2;
            end;
      integer procedure G(X,Z);
            G := (X + Z)↑2;
      A := 1;
      A := G(A,F(A));
      print (A)
end
```

Example 2.23 Averaging 10 Numbers in BASIC and "Extended" BASIC

2.23a. Poor	2.23b. Better
10 S = 0	10 LET S = 0
20 FOR I = 1 TO 10	20 LET N = 10
30 S = S + I	30 FOR I = 1 TO N
40 NEXT I	40 LET S = S + I
50 M = S/(I−1)	50 NEXT I
60 PRINT M	60 LET M = S/N
70 END	70 PRINT M
	80 END

Example 2.23a also exhibits another implementation-dependent feature. For the algorithm to work correctly, the value of I must be 11 in line 50 of the first version. In order for this to occur, the implementation of BASIC must first increment I and exit the loop only when I is greater than 10. Thus when I is 10 and control hits the NEXT statement, I will become 11, I will then be compared with 10, and control will pass to statement 50. The value of M = S/(I−1) will then be 55/10, the correct answer. This is one way BASIC may be implemented.

In a different implementation, I may be checked against 10 *before* I is incremented. If I is less than 10, it will be incremented by 1, and the loop executed. If I is equal to 10, the loop will be exited. This implementation of BASIC is just as valid as the first but gives a different result for M. While the number of iterations is still 10, upon exit the value of I is 10 rather than 11. This makes the value of M = S/(I−1) equal to 55/9, the wrong answer.

In still another implementation, the value of the loop variable I may be undefined after execution. While this may be an annoying (albeit valid) implementation, an unpredictable result would occur in Example 2.23a. The program of 2.23b omits this implementation-dependent feature entirely. It may be run without change on any implementation that supports standard BASIC.

Besides implementation-dependent features of a given language, different languages may have parallel features whose implementations are not identical. For example, many languages allow a programmer to dimension arrays simply by stating the number of elements per subscript. When this is possible, a default convention exists so that subscripts can be used to reference the array elements. The problem here is that these default conventions vary. For example, in PL/I,

DECLARE A(10);

specifies a 10-element array whose subscripts vary from 1 to 10. Other languages have different defaults. Some of these are listed in the following table.

Language	Array Specification	Subscript Range	No. Elements
PL/I	DECLARE A(10)	1:10	10
BASIC	DIM A(10)	1:10 (or 0:10)	10 (or 11)
LISP 1.5	(ARRAY (A (10) LIST))	0:9	10
SNOBOL4	A = ARRAY(10)	1:10	10
MAD	DIMENSION A(10)	0:10	11

If possible, specify the lower bound of your array subscripts so that other readers of your program will not be hindered by ignorance of the default options. It is also a good idea to specify the lower bound to be 1 since 1 is the default lower bound in most languages.

Implementation-dependent features are enticing as time savers and frequently can shorten your program. The reader can probably make a good case for the use of favorite features in a particular implementation. Nevertheless, programmers should be wary of features that could cause problems with another kind of implementation. But if you have good reason to do otherwise, it must be admitted (in this proverb especially) that the exception proves the rule.

Proverb 15   AVOID TRICKS

Every programmer has a secret desire to produce a truly clever program. Shortening the code by two lines, running the program two seconds faster, or using fewer identifiers are all popular pastimes. *Resist this temptation,* because the benefits seldom match the hidden costs. Aside from the extra time needed to develop that "special wrinkle," hand-checking and debugging tricky code is often a study in horror, and one must be extra careful of boundary conditions.

When tricks are indiscriminately employed, good structure, flexibility, and clarity are frequently lost. Merging two or more sections of code to wring out those "extra" lines is an easy method of preventing anyone from following your algorithm or extending your program. Before removing the extra lines, it might be worthwhile to remember that fewer lines of source code may *not* always result in fewer machine instructions.

Consider Example 2.24. Each element of code is designed to select the player leading the first card in a card game. Successively higher bids are represented by successively increasing numbers. BID(n) denotes the final bid of the nth player. The players are numbered clockwise from 1 to 4. The lead player is the person next to the highest bidder. MAX denotes the numerically highest bid made by a player during the bidding. Example 2.24a assumes that testing for equality yields one of two values, 1 (for true) or 0 (for false). This program eliminates one variable and three lines of code. Would you use it for your card-playing program?

Example 2.24   Code to Determine the Player Leading the First Card in a Card Game

---

2.24a. Poor

```
N = (BID(1) = MAX) + 2*(BID(2)  = MAX) + 3*(BID(3) = MAX) + 4*(BID(4) = MAX);

LEAD_PLAYER = 1 + N*SIGN(4-N);
```


2.24b. Better

```
DO PLAYER = 1 BY 1 TO 4;
      IF BID(PLAYER) = MAX THEN DECLARER = PLAYER;
END;

IF DECLARER = 4 THEN LEAD_PLAYER = 1;
              ELSE LEAD_PLAYER = DECLARER + 1;
```

If you do prefer the program of 2.24a to that of 2.24b, look at both examples carefully. Do you prefer the first because it executes more rapidly or requires less storage? On the computer you regularly use, you may in fact find that Example 2.24b requires less storage, because the loop may take fewer instructions than the straightline code from the corresponding statement in 2.24a. In addition, example 2.24b may execute faster because no divisions or multiplications are required, and there may be fewer additions. In short, beware of "clever" code, and beware of being "penny wise" but "pound foolish."

For a more complete discussion of this topic, see the section of Chapter 4 entitled "Representation of Algorithms and Tricky Programming."

Proverb 16   BUILD IN DEBUGGING TECHNIQUES

Nobody's perfect. When writing your program, prepare for the worst. If you include a new major procedure, have a provision to test it separately.

When you first run a major section of code and control changes to another section of the program, make sure that control goes to the correct place. Although Chapter 4 contains a more elaborate discussion of debugging aids, we will briefly make the point here.

Strategic locations for debugging aids will suggest themselves while you are writing the program. If you intitially spare a few moments to insert debugging aids, you will save time in the long run. Otherwise, if there is an aborted run (optimists get only unpleasant surprises), having to go back over the program to find the best places for debugging aids will take much longer and be less fruitful. When the program is running correctly, it takes only a few seconds to remove the debugging sections (if they need to be removed). If the structure of your program precludes debugging code, then it may be worth rewriting the program.

What can be used as a debugging aid? That depends upon your language and system. PL/I has numerous facilities for checking error conditions that arise during program execution. Standard ALGOL 60 has no direct debugging aids. As for other languages, LISP 1.5 has facilities for tracing calls and breaking out of loops, and SNOBOL4 has elaborate tracing facilities.

Many system implementations have facilities beyond those given in the language. Know what features your system provides, and incorporate them into your program. Although it may not be wise to use implementation-dependent features as part of your program, it would be foolish to omit them from debugging.

There is one important debugging aid in all languages and all systems. In computer lingo it is sometimes known as a "selective dump"; technically, it is known as the PRINT statement. PRINT statements can provide snapshots of the program at any point. Use them generously for debugging purposes. For procedures you can position PRINT statements just before or after the calls, as illustrated in Example 2.25. In addition, it is frequently helpful to make the first executable statement in the procedure a PRINT statement that prints the procedure name. For checking the path of control through the program, moreover, place a PRINT statement with a counter variable at selected points.

Example 2.25   Use of PRINT Statement as a Debugging Aid

2.25a. No Debugging Aids	2.25b. With Debugging Aids
PL/I	PL/I

```
2.25a. No Debugging Aids           2.25b.  With Debugging Aids

         PL/I                              PL/I

MAJOR_SUB:  PROCEDURE (X,Y,Z);     MAJOR_SUB:  PROCEDURE (X,Y,Z);
    .                                  .
    .                                  .
END MAJOR_SUB;                     END MAJOR_SUB;
    .                                  .
    .                                  .
CALL MAJOR_SUB (A,B,C);            PUT LIST ('A,B,C ARE', A,B,C);
                                   CALL MAJOR_SUB (A,B,C);
                                   PUT LIST ('AFTER MAJOR_SUB, A,B,C, ARE', A,B,C);
```

Example 2.25   Use of PRINT Statement as a Debugging Aid (cont'd)

ALGOL 60	ALGOL 60

```
procedure  MAJORSUB(X,Y,Z);        procedure  MAJORSUB(X,Y,Z);
   .                                   .
   .                                   .
end MAJORSUB;                       end MAJORSUB;
   .                                   .
   .                                   .
MAJORSUB (A,B,C);                   print ('A,B,C ARE', A,B,C);
                                   MAJORSUB(A,B,C);
                                   print ('AFTER MAJORSUB A,B,C ARE', A,B,C);
```

Finally, position debugging statements to check any difficult algorithms or any variable whose value you are uncertain of. Debugging techniques are a programmer's best friend. Use them!

Proverb 17   NEVER ASSUME THE COMPUTER ASSUMES ANYTHING

A computer is like a malevolent genius. If you don't tell it what to do, it won't do it. So long as you give precise instructions, the results will be what you expect; the moment you get careless, however, the results will become unpredictable. If you say "add something to X" and you have not specified what that "something" is, watch out. The computer will either stop immediately or use the first thing it can find!

Two common errors, caused by failure to initialize variables, are illustrated in Examples 2.26 and 2.27. In Example 2.26a, the statement sequence to print

Example 2.26   Failure to Initialize a Variable

2.26a. Wrong	2.26b. Right

PL/I	PL/I

```
DO I = 1 TO 100;          S = 0;
   S = S + I;             DO I = 1 TO 100;
END;                          S = S + I;
PUT LIST(S/100);          END;
                          PUT LIST(S/100)
```

ALGOL 60	ALGOL 60

```
for I := 1 step 1 until 100 do    S := 0;
   S := S + I;                    for I := 1 step 1 until 100 do
print (S/100);                        S  = S + I;
                                  print (S/100);
```

Example 2.27   Failure to Place Initialization in Proper Place

2.27a. Wrong	2.27b. Right

PL/I (left)

```
S = 0;
DO N = 10 BY 10 TO 100;
    DO I = 1 BY 1 TO N;
        S = S + I;
    END;
    PUT LIST('AVERAGE IS',S/N);
END;
```

PL/I (right)

```
DO N = 10 BY 10 TO 100;
    S = 0;
    DO I = 1 BY 1 TO N;
        S = S + I;
    END;
    PUT LIST('AVERAGE IS',S/N);
END;
```

ALGOL 60 (left)

```
S := 0;
for N := 10 step 10 until 100 do
begin
    for I := 1 step 1 until N do
        S = S + I;
    print ('AVERAGE IS', S/N);
end
```

ALGOL 60 (right)

```
for N := 10 step 10 until 100 do
begin
    S := 0;
    for I := 1 step 1 until N do
        S = S + I;
    print ('AVERAGE IS', S/N);
end
```

out the average of the first 100 positive integers may generate an error because the initial value of S has not been specified. Consider also the programs in Example 2.27, which are meant to print out the averages of the first N positive integers, for N = 10, 20, . . ., 100. Merely placing the initialization of S somewhere before its value is used, as in Example 2.27a, is insufficient. Care must be taken regarding the location of the initialization. Because S is not reset to 0 for each iteration of the outer loop, the first program gives incorrect results. This error is remedied in Example 2.27b.

Numbers are not the only quantities that require careful initialization. Example 2.28 shows an initialization error in a string manipulation program. The program is intended to read in a sequence of character strings and to print each string in reverse order. The program terminates when the input string is an asterisk. We assume an integer-valued function subprogram LENGTH that returns the number of initial nonblank characters contained in the array given as an argument. We also assume that a single storage unit can hold six characters. Do you see the problem and how to correct it *without reading on?*

Upon each iteration of the algorithm, the array REVERS retains the value of the previous string. This causes an input-dependent error, which occurs only when a new string is shorter than a previous string. This error is particularly difficult to detect with the sample input/output of Example 2.28. The cause of the error was the (probably unsuspected) assumption that the value of REVERS would be reset to null merely because the programmer was no longer interested in the previous value. The correction required is to place the initialization of REVERS later in the program.

Example 2.28   Failure to Initialize a String Variable in BASIC

```
(Program)

        INTEGER STRING(80), REVERS(80), HALT, BLANKS
        DATA   HALT/6H*       /, BLANKS/6H          /
C
        DO 10   I = 1,80
   10      REVERS(I) = BLANKS
C
   20 READ(5,100) STRING
        IF (STRING(1) .EQ. HALT) STOP
        L = LENGTH(STRING)
        DO 30   I = 1,L
        K          = L - I + 1
   30      REVERS(K) = STRING(I)
C
        WRITE(6,200) STRING,REVERS
        GOTO 20
C
  100 FORMAT (80A1)
  200 FORMAT (1H , 80A1 / 1H , 15X, 80A1)
        END


(Input/Output)


THE
                EHT
PROGRAMMING
                GNIMMARGORP
PROVERBS
                SBREVORPORP
```

More generally, a programmer should be careful to know in detail the
default conventions of any particular implementation. When in doubt, never
assume that the computer assumes anything. Careful initialization may avoid
many unfortunate errors or prevent an unnecessary machine dependency.

Proverb 18   USE COMMENTS

Comments are a form of internal documentation that allows the programmer to describe the program from within. They are invaluable for illuminating
the logical structure of a program and as reference points for making documentation. One example will suffice to make the point. Whether or not you know the
BASIC language, considers the program of Example 2.29a. This program represents the ultimate in obscurity, a program with no comments. The reader is
invited to examine the program and determine the meaning of each statement.

Example 2.29 Two BASIC Programs to Compute Greatest Common Divisors

2.29a. Poor

```
10    PRINT "A", "B", "G.C.D."
20    READ N
30    FOR I = 1 TO N
40         READ A,B
50         PRINT A,B,
60         LET Q = INT(A/B)
70         LET R = A - Q*B
80         LET A = B
90         LET B = R
100        IF R > 0 THEN 60
110        PRINT A
120   NEXT I
130   STOP
140   DATA 3
150   DATA 36,6,130,169,100,99
160   END
```

2.29b. Better

```
10    REM          A PROGRAM TO FIND THE GREATEST COMMON DIVISORS
20    REM          OF N PAIRS OF NUMBERS USING EUCLID'S ALGORITHM.
30    REM          WRITTEN BY EDWINA J. CARTER 7/8/72.
40    REM
50    REM /* PRINT HEADINGS */
60         PRINT "A", "B", "G.C.D."
70    REM
80         READ N
90         FOR I = 1 TO N
100   REM
110              /* READ AND PRINT VALUES OF A AND B */
120              READ A,B
130              PRINT A,B,
140   REM
150   REM        /* USE EUCLID'S ALGORITHM */
160              LET Q = INT(A/B)
170              LET R = A - Q*B
180              LET A = B
190              LET B = R
200   REM
210   REM        /* IF DIVISOR IS NOT FOUND, REPEAT; OTHERWISE PRINT RESULTS */
220              IF R > 0 THEN 160
230              PRINT A
240         NEXT I
250         STOP
260   REM
270         DATA 3
280         DATA 36,6,130,169,100,99
290         END
```

Next consider the program of Example 2.29b. The comments contain a store of information. They convey the logical structure of the program and even tell us who is to blame if an error develops. This information is particularly valuable to someone who is using the program without a copy of the documentation or to someone who doesn't want to spend any excess time trying to figure out the program.

Although the value of using comments can be illustrated over and over again, the programmer is often tempted not to use them. After all, when a programmer is writing a piece of code, he doesn't really need the comments. But how many times during coding does the programmer go back to try to figure out what he has done and what is left to do? And what about the next day? Or the next week? Or the occasion when the programmer or someone else may be asked to change the program? In short, comments may be exactly what is needed.

One additional proverb is useful here: *Temperance is moderation in all things.* Comments can be overused as well as misused. Comments do require extra time for printing and extra storage space. Furthermore, it is a bad idea to comment every other line. Comments should convey useful information. A situation such as the following:

$$/* \text{ COMMENT: A GETS B PLUS C } */$$
$$A = B + C$$

not only clutters up your program but may completely discourage anyone trying to wade through it. In short, comments are there for your convenience. They can really make a difference. *Use them, temperately.*

Proverb 19   PRETTYPRINT

If there is one proverb in the book that is simple to follow yet enormously effective, this is it. Few languages require strict column formatting of programs. More often, free format is the watchword. Free format means that spacing is ignored, expressions may be arbitrarily spaced, or statements may be split over several lines. It allows the programmer great flexibility in writing his program. The spacing of programs to illuminate their logical structure is known as "prettyprinting." Even languages like FORTRAN that place some restrictions on statement format are usually sufficiently flexible to allow indenting and spacing.

Parallel sections of code should each be indented to the same margin. Inner blocks of code, such as the bodies of loops, procedures, or IF statements, should be indented further. Liberal use should be made of blank spaces and blank lines. Borrowing from a previous example, Example 2.30 shows PL/I and ALGOL 60 statement sequences unspaced and their corresponding prettyprinted versions. The gain in clarity of the prettyprinted versions is unquestionable.

There may be languages which do not allow such spacing. In addition, there are times when such spacing is not desirable. In these circumstances, other

Example 2.30   Use of Spacing in PL/I and ALGOL 60

2.30a.   Poor

```
    PL/I                                            ALGOL 60

DO PLAYER = 1 BY 1 TO 4;                    for PLAYER := 1 step 1 until 4
IF BID(PLAYER) = MAX                        do if BID(PLAYER) = MAX
THEN DECLARER = PLAYER;   END;              then DECLARER := PLAYER; if
IF DECLARER = 4 THEN LEAD_PLAYER = 1;       DECLARER = 4 then   LEADPLAYER   := 1
ELSE LEAD_PLAYER = DECLARER + 1;            else LEADPLAYER := DECLARER + 1;
```

2.30b.   Better

```
    PL/I                                            ALGOL 60

DO PLAYER = 1 BY 1 TO 4;                    for PLAYER := 1 step 1 until 4 do
   IF BID(PLAYER) = MAX                        if BID(PLAYER) = MAX
      THEN DECLARER = PLAYER;                     then DECLARER := PLAYER;
END;
                                           if DECLARER = 4
IF DECLARER = 4                               then LEADPLAYER := 1
   THEN LEAD_PLAYER = 1;                       else LEADPLAYER := DECLARER + 1;
   ELSE LEAD_PLAYER = DECLARER + 1;
```

methods can and should be used to illuminate the structure of your program. In any case, the moral is the same. If your program has a good logical structure, show it. For a more complete discussion, see the section on "Prettyprinting" in Chapter 4.

Proverb 20   PROVIDE GOOD DOCUMENTATION

Once a program is working perfectly, it is seldom the case that the programmer's task is ended. The programmer may be asked to write a report on the program, summarize it for his manager, submit it for evaluation, modify it, or give it to others for their use. For any of these purposes, good documentation must be provided.

While the need for documentation is clear, the absence of standards for documentation is unfortunate. The following guidelines may be helpful. For one, at the top level, the programmer should briefly state the input/output characteristics of his program. For example, consider the following description.

Program name: ALPHA

Input: A positive integer N; an array A containing N integers

Output: The mean and standard deviation of the N elements in the array A

Special conditions: If all elements are 0, then "ERROR" is printed

At this level the programmer should not provide detailed explanations of the inner workings of his program, but rather describe only the input to his program, its output, and the effects of any unusual conditions.

Further documentation of a program should include a similar description of subprograms, a flow chart of critical algorithms, a description of vital data structures, and an explanation of the input/output format. For many programs, it is a good idea to provide a list of key variables and their uses, especially programs written in languages that allow only short identifiers, such as BASIC.

It is critical that the documentation be well-structured. A reader who wishes a specific depth of detail should be able to obtain exactly the information he needs, *no more* and *no less.*

Two common pitfalls in documenting are providing too little information and providing too much. There is little excuse for skimping in the documentation; if you are going to document at all, you might as well be complete. On the other hand, providing too much information can totally obscure the intent of the documentation in the first place. There is a tendency for a programmer, especially after spending many hours at his task, to describe unnecessary details, such as the use of insignificant variables, trivial algorithms, unimportant or commonplace data structures, and so forth. Often this level of detail serves only as a distraction from the critical information.

In brief, document (that is, explain) a program up to the point at which the program structure and comments can effectively take over. Document wisely. You will be glad you did.

Proverb 21   HAND-CHECK THE PROGRAM BEFORE RUNNING IT

It can be difficult to convince a programmer that he should hand-check his program before running it. Yet run-time errors are the hardest to detect, and unless the system provides excellent debugging facilities, using the computer to help is full of hazards. Even in a time-sharing environment, the programmer is well-advised to check out every program completely by hand *before* running it. He may well be surprised at the errors he catches, for example, errors like incorrect signs, infinite loops, and program crashes.

The technique is simple. Choose a sample input, then calculate the output as if *you* were the computer—assuming nothing and using *exactly* what is written. See that each logical unit performs correctly and that the control sequence through the units is correct. If the program is too long or complex to check in its entirety, then check each major section first, and later check the smaller units, assuming that the major sections are correct.

When choosing sample input, take special care to include the boundary conditions and other special cases. Failure to account for these is one of the most common programming errors. For example, suppose you were asked to write a program that takes two nonnegative integers as input, a dividend and a divisor, and prints out two numbers, the integer part of the quotient and the integer remainder.

Assume that your system does not have a built-in function like FLOOR in PL/I, which gives the integer part of a floating-point number, or an integer division operator like ÷ in ALGOL 60. That is, assume that you cannot just say:

PL/I

QUOTIENT = FLOOR (DIVIDEND/DIVISOR);
REMAINDER = DIVIDEND − QUOTIENT*DIVISOR;

ALGOL 60

QUOTIENT   := DIVIDEND ÷ DIVISOR;
REMAINDER := DIVIDEND − QUOTIENT*DIVISOR;

As a first pass, consider the program given in two languages in Example 2.31a. Does it work? Obviously it doesn't, for if it did, it wouldn't be in a section called "Check Your Program before Running It." Checking by hand, we find that it bombs out because REMAINDER is initially undefined. (Remember? Never assume that the computer assumes anything.) So we change the program to that shown in Example 2.31b.

Does the program work now? Obviously not, or we wouldn't have asked.

Example 2.31   Hand-Checking a Program

2.31a   First Attempt

PL/I

```
GET LIST (DIVIDEND, DIVISOR);

DO QUOTIENT = 0 BY 1 WHILE (REMAINDER > DIVISOR);
   REMAINDER = REMAINDER - DIVISOR;
END;

PUT LIST (QUOTIENT, REMAINDER);
```

ALGOL 60

```
read (DIVIDEND, DIVISOR);

QUOTIENT := -1;
for QUOTIENT := QUOTIENT +1 while (REMAINDER > DIVISOR) do
    REMAINDER := REMAINDER - DIVISOR;

print (QUOTIENT, REMAINDER);
```

2.31b. Second Attempt.

PL/I

```
GET LIST  (DIVIDEND, DIVISOR);

REMAINDER = DIVIDEND;
DO  QUOTIENT = 0 BY 1 WHILE (REMAINDER > DIVISOR);
    REMAINDER = REMAINDER - DIVISOR;
END;

PUT LIST (QUOTIENT, REMAINDER);
```

ALGOL 60

```
read (DIVIDEND, DIVISOR);

REMAINDER := DIVIDEND;
QUOTIENT  := -1;
for  QUOTIENT := QUOTIENT +1  while (REMAINDER > DIVISOR) do
     REMAINDER := REMAINDER - DIVISOR;

print (QUOTIENT,REMAINDER);
```

2.31c. Third Attempt

PL/I

```
GET LIST (DIVIDEND, DIVISOR);
IF DIVISOR = 0
THEN BEGIN;
     PUT LIST('DIVISION BY 0');
     STOP;
END;

REMAINDER = DIVIDEND;
DO QUOTIENT  = 0 BY 1 WHILE (REMAINDER > DIVISOR);
   REMAINDER = REMAINDER - DIVISOR;
END;

PUT LIST(QUOTIENT, REMAINDER);
```

ALGOL 60

```
read (DIVIDEND,DIVISOR);
if  DIVISOR = 0
then begin
     print ('DIVISION BY 0');
     stop;
end;

REMAINDER := DIVIDEND;
QUOTIENT  := -1;
for  QUOTIENT := QUOTIENT +1  while (REMAINDER > DIVISOR) do
     REMAINDER := REMAINDER - DIVISOR;

print (QUOTIENT,REMAINDER);
```

2.31d. Fourth Attempt

PL/I

```
GET LIST (DIVIDEND, DIVISOR);
IF DIVISOR = 0
THEN BEGIN;
     PUT LIST('DIVISION BY 0');
     STOP;
END;

REMAINDER = DIVIDEND;
DO QUOTIENT = 0 BY 1 WHILE (REMAINDER >=  DIVISOR);
   REMAINDER = REMAINDER - DIVISOR;
END;

PUT LIST(QUOTIENT,REMAINDER);
```

ALGOL 60

```
read (DIVIDEND,DIVISOR),
if  DIVISOR = 0
then begin
     print ('DIVISION BY 0');
     stop;
end;

REMAINDER := DIVIDEND;
QUOTIENT   := -1;
for QUOTIENT := QUOTIENT +1 while (REMAINDER ≥ DIVISOR) do
     REMAINDER := REMAINDER - DIVISOR;

print (QUOTIENT,REMAINDER);
```

Checking the boundary conditions by hand, we find that when the divisor is zero, the algorithm doesn't terminate. Since division by zero is undefined, we should process this case separately. It wouldn't be wise to leave the program in an infinite loop, computer time costing what it does. We thus change the program as shown in Example 2.31c.

It still doesn't work. Checking another boundary condition, we find that if the divisor exactly divides the dividend, we always get a quotient of 1 less than the correct value. For example, 10 divided by 5 is 2 with a remainder of 0, not 1 with a remainder of 5. Correcting this error is easy, as shown by Example 2.31d.

This version works. Although the first error probably would have been picked up easily at run time, the other two probably would not have been. Their effects are input-dependent. Can you imagine searching for a data-dependent error in a long program that goes bad only once in a while?

Simply stated, check your program (especially the boundary conditions) before running it.

Proverb 22   GET THE PROGRAM CORRECT BEFORE TRYING TO PRODUCE GOOD OUTPUT

The primary consideration in programming is to obtain a correct running program. Secondary considerations are structure and efficiency. Providing elaborate output should be deferred until other, more important considerations have been taken care of. The most elaborate, clever, and aesthetic output is unimpressive if the program itself is wrong. Similarly, it is unwise to finalize your output if the structure of your program is likely to change for reasons of efficiency or clarity. Producing good output is desirable but should wait its turn in the hierarchy of programming priorities.

So do not spend your time initially thinking of lovely output. Concentrate on the computations. Get your program correct first. Later you can concentrate on good output.

Proverb 23   WHEN THE PROGRAM IS CORRECT, PRODUCE GOOD OUTPUT

Proverb 23 dutifully follows from Proverb 22. Any experienced programmer engaged in writing programs for use by others knows that, once his program is working correctly, good output is a must. Few people really care how much time and trouble a programmer has spent in designing and debugging a program. Most people see only the results. Often, by the time a programmer has finished tackling a difficult problem, any output may look great. The programmer knows what it means and how to interpret it. However, the same cannot be said for others, or even for the programmer himself six months hence.

The point is obvious. After all that work and effort spent in writing a program, don't let it look slipshod by having messy, poorly spaced, or skimpy output. Consider Example 2.32a. The output of this program would be incomprehensible without an exact knowledge of the problem definition or the program itself. The output of the program of Example 2.32b, on the other hand, can be clearly understood by anyone.

The moral is simple. When your program is working, annotate your output so that its meaning can stand on its own.

Proverb 24   REREAD THE MANUAL

Now why would anyone want to go back and read that boring language manual again? A wise programmer will occasionally do exactly that and will sometimes be pleasantly surprised to find out what he learns. After programming for a while, a programmer tends to restrict himself to a convenient subset of his language. As a result, many useful constructs may be forgotten. Periodically rereading the manual will help to keep these constructs in mind when the need arises.

If you are an ALGOL programmer, do you know the (somewhat confusing) rules for the placing of semicolons and comments? Do you know the subtleties of call-by-name and call-by-value, and their effect on the evaluation of recursive procedures? Can you give two expressions, e_1 and e_2, such that the value of $e_1 + e_2$ is different from $e_2 + e_1$?

If you program in PL/I, do you know how to use all of the editing features for output format? Do you know all the different ways of "factoring out" attributes in DECLARE statements and the uses of all the various attributes?

If you are a FORTRAN programmer, do you know how FORTRAN deals with character strings and the A format? Do you know the cases where INTEGER and REAL quantities can be combined without a mixed mode error?

If you are familiar with BASIC, do you remember the order in which data

Example 2.32 Use of Informative Output

2.32a. Poor	2.32b. Better
(Program)	(Program)

```
P: PROCEDURE;
   DECLARE AMT_SOLD(1:4) FIXED,
      SALESMAN_NO FIXED;

   GET LIST (SALESMAN_NO);
   PUT LIST (SALESMAN_NO);
   GET LIST (AMT_SOLD);
   DO J = 1 TO 4;
      PUT LIST(AMT_SOLD(J)) SKIP;
   END;

   PUT LIST(SUM(AMT_SOLD)/4) SKIP;
END P;
```

```
P: PROCEDURE;
   DECLARE AMT_SOLD(1:4) FIXED,
      SALESMAN_NO FIXED;

   GET LIST (SALESMAN_NO);
   PUT EDIT ('SALESMAN', SALESMAN_NO,
         ' SOLD ') (A, P'Z9999', A);
   GET LIST (AMT_SOLD);
   DO J = 1 TO 4;
   PUT EDIT(AMT_SOLD(J),' IN WEEK ',J)
         (X(5), P'$$$$9', A, P'9')
         SKIP;
   END;

   PUT EDIT ('AVERAGE WEEKLY SALES ',
         SUM(AMT_SOLD)/4)
         (A, P'$$$$9') SKIP;
END P;
```

(Data)

2704, 1030,   980, 1000,   990

(Data)

2704, 1030,   980, 1000,   990

(Output)

```
2704
1030
980
1000
990
1000
```

(Output)

```
SALESMAN 2704 SOLD
     $1030 IN WEEK 1
      $980 IN WEEK 2
     $1000 IN WEEK 3
      $990 IN WEEK 4
AVERAGE WEEKLY SALES $1000
```

items have to be entered for a MAT READ statement? Do you know all the predefined mathematical functions and the file manipulation capabilities?

In general, do you know the implementation-dependent depth to which you can nest loops, conditionals, or program blocks? How about the number of significant figures kept by your particular machine? In short, if a programmer discovers a new feature, he should ask, "When would I use it?" If he does, he may be pleased to find the results.

Proverb 25   CONSIDER ANOTHER LANGUAGE

There are many computer languages. Many of them are special-purpose languages that are especially useful for certain classes of problems. There are languages devised to process strings, like SNOBOL4; languages to manipulate lists, such as LISP; and languages for vector and matrix manipulation, such as APL. If you were asked to write a program to input a string of characters and remove all of the blanks, you could use PL/I or BASIC and write:

```
                PL/I                                      BASIC

DECLARE STRING CHARACTER(72) VARYING;     100  DIM S$(72),T$(72)
GET EDIT(STRING) (A);                     110  FOR I = 1 TO 72
DO I = INDEX(STRING,' ') WHILE I >= 1;    120    T$(I) = ' '
   SUBSTR(STRING,I,1) = '';               130  NEXT I
END;                                      140  INPUT S$
PUT EDIT(STRING) (A);                     150  LET J = 0
                                          160  FOR I = 1 TO LEN(SS)
                                          170    IF S$(I) = ' '  THEN 200
                                          180    LET J = J + 1
                                          190    LET T$(J) = S$(I)
                                          200  NEXT I
                                          210  MAT PRINT T$;
```

whereas in SNOBOL4 you could write:

```
                     SNOBOL

         STRING      = TRIM(INPUT)
   ZAP   STRING ' '  = NULL        :S(ZAP)
         OUTPUT      = STRING
```

In practice, most programmers are limited in their choice of languages for one or more of the following reasons:

(1) They may be told to choose a specific language either because they are students in a course using one language, or because they are professionals working in a fixed-language environment.

(2) They may know only one or two languages well enough to make a good choice.

(3) They may have access to a machine that is equipped for only a few languages.

Beyond that, there are not many polylingual programmers fluent in five or six languages. Even these programmers would probably program in the language (a) they like the best, (b) they learned first, or (c) they are working with at the present. So again, there will be some constraint, even if only psychological.

Suffice it to say that, despite these constraints, some other language may be better suited to your problem, and if everything is in your favor, consider that language.

Proverb 26   DON'T BE AFRAID TO START OVER

This is the last proverb but it is of great importance. I dare not dwell on it too long, because I hope you will never have to use it.

A shattered flower vase is often cheaper to replace than to repair. The same is true of computer programs. Repairing a shredded hulk whose structure has been totally destroyed by patches and deletions or a program with a seriously incorrect algorithm just isn't worth the time. The best that could result is a long, inefficient, unintelligible program that defies further change. The worst that could result I dare not think of. When you seem hopelessly in trouble, start over. Lessons painfully learned on the old program can be applied to the new one to yield a better program in far less time with far less trouble.

This last proverb may seem heartless, but don't let your ego stand in the way. Don't be afraid to start over. I mean *really* start over. Scrap the whole thing and begin again.

EXERCISES

Exercise 2.1   (Define the Problem Completely)
Consider the following program specification:

> "Write a program that computes the weight in kilograms of a weight expressed in pounds and ounces."

Upon careful thought, the above specification reveals several points that would be unclear to a programmer. Rewrite the above specification so that any two programs written to solve the problem would have *exactly* the same input/output characteristics, for example, the same input format, the same number of significant digits, the same headings, and so forth. (Note: You are to write a program specification, *not* a program.)

Exercise 2.2 (Define the Problem Completely)

Each of the following program specifications is either missing one or more critical definitions or is written in such a way as to be unclear, misleading, or confusing: (a) How are the program specifications deficient? (b) Rewrite all or part of each program specification to make it as clear and explicit as possible, that is, so that there can be no doubt as to what the program should do. (c) In general, what does *any* program specification require to make it as clear and explicit as possible?

Program Specification 1: Write a program to calculate and print the basic statistics of a set of data.

Program Specification 2: The average cost to fight forest fires in Fortrania is determined by the size of the fire as listed below:

Size	Average Cost to Extinguish
0.75 acres or less	$ 15.00
1.00 acres to 4.75 acres	$ 25.00
5.00 acres to 24.75 acres	$ 50.00
25.00 acres to 99.75 acres	$100.00
Greater than 100 acres	$200.00

Given these rates, write a program to read in a list of fire acreages to two decimal places and then compute the cost to fight them. The output consists of the computed cost labeled with a dollar sign.

Program Specification 3: Given the following rates of payment, write a program that will compute the monthly commission for a car salesman:

Grade of Salesman	Commission Rate
1	$5.00 + .50% for first ten sales $7.50 + .75% every subsequent sale
2	$7.50 + .75% for first ten sales $10.00 + 1.00% every subsequent sale
3	$10.00 + 1.00% for first ten sales $12.50 + 1.25% every subsequent sale
4	$12.50 + 1.25% for first ten sales $15.00 + 1.50% every subsequent sale
5	$15.00 + 1.50% for first ten sales $17.50 + 1.75% every subsequent sale

The input should be the grade of salesman and the number of sales he has made for the month. The output should read "THE SALESMAN'S PAY IS $c," where c is the salesman's commission.

Program Specification 4: The Programmer's Equity Life Insurance Company offers policies of $25,000, $50,000, and $100,000. The cost of a policy holder's annual premium is determined as follows. There is a basic fee that depends upon the amount of coverage carried. This is $25 for a $25,000 policy, $50 for a $50,000 policy, and $100 for a $100,000 policy. In addition to the basic fee, there are two additional charges depending on the age and lifestyle of the policy holder. The first additional charge is determined by multiplying by 2 the policy holder's age minus 21 and then multiplying this by either 1½, 2, or 3 if the policy is at the $25,000, $50,000 or $100,000 level, respectively. The second additional charge is determined by the policy holder's lifestyle, which is a rating of the danger of harm resulting from his occupation and hobbies. This rating is determined by company experts from a questionnaire returned by the policy applicant. They return a rating of from 1 to 5 in steps of 1, with 1 being the safest rating. The charge is then determined by multiplying this rating by 5 and then further multiplying by 1½, 2, or 3 if the policy is either at the $25,000, $50,000 or $100,000 level, respectively. The total premium is found by adding together these separately determined charges. Write a program to output tables of yearly premium costs for men of ages from twenty-one to seventy-five for all amounts of policy value and safety ratings.

Exercise 2.3 (Use Procedures)
Consider a program with the following specification:

> *input:* a positive integer N
> *output:* the values N!, N!!, N!!!, and N!!!!

where N! denotes the factorial of N.
(a) Write the program *without* the use of procedures, functions, or subroutines.
(b) Write the program using procedures, functions, or subroutines. The differences can be quite striking.

Exercise 2.4 (Avoid Unnecessary GOTO's)
Restructure the following statement sequence to eliminate all GOTO's and statement labels and to make the sequence as *short* and clear as possible. (Note: It can be done with only two assignment statements.)

```
              goto L3;
        L1:   if X=0 then goto L9;
              goto L5;
        L5:   if X > 402 then goto L6;
              goto L4;
        L9:   print (X);
              stop;
        L3:   input (X);
              goto L1;
        L6:   X := sqrt (X);
        L8:   X := X↑2 + X;
              goto L9;
        L4:   X := X↑2;
              goto L8;
```

Exercise 2.5 (Avoid Unnecessary GOTO's)

Consider the conventional 8 by 8 array representation of a chess board, whose squares are denoted by (1,1), (1,2), . . ., (8,8), and the problem of placing eight queens on the board so that *no* queen can capture *any other* queen. In chess, a queen can capture another piece if the queen lies on the same row, column, or diagonal as the other piece.

(a) Write a program to read in the coordinates of eight queens and print "TRUE" if no queen can capture any other and "FALSE" otherwise.

(b) Draw a flow diagram for the program according to the form given in Figures 2.1 and 2.2, that is, designating all forward GOTO's with lines on the right and all backward GOTO's with lines on the left.

(c) Score the program according to the following rule: SCORE = 100 − 10*(number of crossing lines). (NOTE: The scores for Figures 2.1 and 2.2 are 70 and 100.)

Exercise 2.6 (Get the Syntax Correct Now, Not Later)

It is important that a programmer be able to detect simple syntactic errors. Consider the following program to compute PI using the series,

$$PI^4/96 = 1/1^4 + 1/3^4 + 1/5^4 \ldots.$$

How many syntactic errors are there? Correct the program so that there are no errors.

```
P:   PROCEDURE OPTIONS(MAIN);
     /* PROCEDURE TO COMPUTE PI */
     DCL (SUM, TEMP) FLOAT,
         N FIXED,
         PI PICTURE '9.999B999B999' FLOAT
     N = 0;
     DO N = N+1 WHILE ABS(TEMP)>1E-10;
         TEMP = 1/(2N-1)**4;
         SUM = SUM + TEMP;
     END;
```

```
                    PI = SQRT(SQRT(96*SUM));
                    PUT LIST (PI);
            END;
```

Exercise 2.7 (Get the Syntax Correct Now, Not Later)
Which of the following examples are syntactically correct instances of the
given ALGOL 60 categories? Correct the erroneous examples. If possible,
you should assume any suitable declarations needed to make a construct
correct. (Note: This exercise contains some subtle syntactic points.)

(a)   *Procedure Declaration:*

procedure F(X,Y);
       for K := 1 step 1 until N do S := S + X[K] − Y[K]

(b)   *Procedure Declaration:*

procedure F(X,Y); integer X,Y; value X,Y;
       A := X↑X + X↑Y

(c)   *Procedure Declaration:*

procedure F(X,Y); integer X,Y;
       A := if X > Y then X − Y else Y − X;
       B := A↑2

(d)   *Procedure Declaration:*

procedure F(X,Y)

(e)   *Arithmetic Expression:*

if B(I) > 1 then 4

(f)   *Expression:*

if if X then Y else Z

(g)   *Statement:*

begin X := Y;
       F(X)
end

(h)   *Statement:*

for I = A step B until C do begin X[I] := A;
                                 Y[I] := A;
                             end

(i)   Statement:

A[I] := F(X) := 1

(j)   *Statement*

        X := F(F);

(k)   *Program*

        begin
                begin integer X;
                    Y := 1;
                    X := Y + 4
                end;
        end

(l)   *Program*

        begin integer X,Y;
            Y := 1;
            begin boolean array X[1:5];
                X[Y] := true
            end;
            X := 1
        end

Exercise 2.8   (Use Good Mnemonic Names)

The following program performs a well-known, simple arithmetic computation. By basically changing all identifiers, rewrite the program so that it
clearly illuminates the intended computation.

```
                FIVE  := 2;
                FOUR  := 4;
    OMAHA:      input (LEFT, MIDDLE, RIGHT);
                if LEFT = 0 then stop;
                RIGHT1   := LEFT*RIGHT*FOUR;
                LEFT1    := MIDDLE*MIDDLE - RIGHT1;
                LEFT2    := sqrt (LEFT1);
                ONE      := (LEFT2 - MIDDLE)/(FIVE*LEFT);
                ANOTHER := - (LEFT2 + MIDDLE)/(2*LEFT);
                print (ONE, ANOTHER);
                goto OMAHA;
```

Exercise 2.9   (Leave Loop Variables Alone)

What is printed by the following statements? (Note: This exercise is quite
difficult.)

PL/I

```
X = 0;
I = 0;
J = 0;
```

ALGOL 60

```
X := 0;
I := 0;
J := 0;
```

```
DO I = J + 1 TO I + 100;              for I := J + 1 step 1 until I + 100 do
  DO J = I + 1 TO J + 10;                 for J := I + 1 step 1 until J + 10 do
    I = J - 1;                              begin I := J - 1;
    X = X + 1;                                    X := X + 1;
  END;                                      end;
END;                                     print(X);
PUT LIST(X);
```

Exercise 2.10 (Do Not Recompute Constants in a Loop)

Consider a program to compute the gravitational force F exerted between two planets M_1 and M_2 located (over time) at different orbital distances from each other. In particular, let

$$M_1 \; = \; \text{mass of planet 1} = 6 \times 10^{24}$$
$$M_2 \; = \; \text{mass of planet 2} = 8 \times 10^{25}$$
$$G \; \; = \; \text{gravitational constant} = 6.7 \times 10^{-11}$$
$$F \; \; = \; G * M_1 * M_2 / (R \uparrow 2)$$

Write a program to output F for values of R varying from $100 * 10^8$ to $110 * 10^8$ in increments of $.01 * 10^8$ such that *no* constant terms are recomputed.

Exercise 2.11 (When Your Program is Correct, Produce Good Output)

The following input/output was generated by the use of a working program in a time-sharing environment:

input:	WHAT IS N1 AND N2?	
	5,10	
output:	5	25
	6	36
	7	49
	8	64
	9	81
	10	100

Rewrite the input/output so that the average "man on the street" would be able to understand what the input numbers 5 and 10 represent and what the output means.

Exercise 2.12 (Reread the Manual)

There are *no* syntactic errors in the following PL/I structure declaration. Draw a *labeled* tree representing the actual structure defined in the declaration and show *every* element. (Note: Unless you know PL/I very well, this exercise is more difficult than it appears.)

```
DECLARE   1    UNALIGNED,
          3    BINARY (3),
               7    FIXED DECIMAL (3,2),
          4    FINAL BINARY FIXED,
          2       INITIAL (1,3),
          3    (CHARACTER, STRING(5), VARYING);
```

Exercise 2.13 (Reread the Manual)

Answer precisely the following questions with reference to your favorite language: (a) What are the spacing conventions that enable or prohibit prettyprinting? (b) How many dimensions may an array have? (c) What is a legal subscript? (d) What are the logical values of the language (that is, the values representing *true* and *false*)? (e) Are matrix commands available? (f) Does the language allow recursion? (g) Is multiple assignment allowed?

Exercise 2.14 (Several Proverbs)

The following program performs a simple, well-known computation. Rewrite the program so that it clearly illuminates the intended computation. In the process, avoid unnecessary GOTO's (Proverb 7), use mnemonic names (Proverb 10), and produce good output (Proverb 23).

```
P:   PROCEDURE OPTIONS(MAIN);
          GO TO L1;
     L2:  GET LIST(A);
          F = A*A;
          GO TO L3;
     L1:  GET LIST(B);
          G = B*B;
          GO TO L2;
     L3:  IF (A <= 0 | B <= 0)
          THEN GO TO L1;
          C = F + G;
          D = SQRT(C);
          PUT LIST(D);
     END P;
```

Exercise 2.15 (Several Proverbs)

The following procedure is supposed to have the following characteristics:

input: a sequence of non-zero integers terminated by the integer zero.
output: the MEAN

$$(\sum_{i=1}^{n} x_i) / n$$

and standard deviation,

$$\mathrm{SQRT}(\,(\sum_{i=1}^{n} x_i^2)/n - \mathrm{MEAN}^2\,)$$

of the integers in the input sequence.

```
P:   PROCEDURE;
DCL FIXED (A,B,C);
DCL FLOAT (D,E,F);

     A = B = C = 0;
     D = E = F = 0.0;
     L2:  GET LIST (G);
             IF G = 0 THEN GO TO L1;
             A = A+G;
             B = B+1;
             C = C+G**2;
             IF (G>F) THEN F = G;
             GOTO L2;
             D = A/B;
             E = (C/B-A**2)**(1/2);
             I = F - D/F;
     L1:  PUT LIST (D,E);
END P;
```

Of the 26 programming proverbs, which *single* proverb, if properly followed, would be most valuable in converting the above program to a good program? (Note: There really *is* a best answer.)

Exercise 2.16 (Several Proverbs)

Write a program that determines whether an input string is a palindrome. A palindrome is a string that reads the same forwards and backwards. For example, LEVEL is a palindrome while PALINDROME is not. When the program is running correctly, score the program with the following formula:

SCORE = 100 − 5*TIMES_RESUBMITTED − 2*NUMBER_OF_ERRORS

Exercise 2.17 (An ALGOL 60 Quiz and a PL/I Quiz)

A user who has a *very thorough* knowledge of his language should be able to detect erroneus programs that prematurely terminate because of a syntactic (compile-time) or semantic (run-time) error. In the absence of a formal definition of a language, the definition of constructs that produce fatal syntactic or semantic errors must ultimately be based on a particular implementation. To treat this issue precisely, consider the insertion of print statements as the first and last executable statements in a program, and let us adopt the following definitions:

(a)   A program is "syntactically incorrect" if the first print statement is not executed, that is, the compiler finds an unacceptable error.

(b)   A program is "syntactically correct" if the first print statement is executed, that is, the compiler detects no severe errors, translates the program into machine language, and begins execution.

(c)   A program is "semantically incorrect" (but syntactically correct) if the first but not the last print statement is executed, that is, the program is compiled and execution is started but not completed.

(d)   A program is "semantically correct" (and syntactically correct) if the first and last print statements are executed, that is, the program is compiled and executed without abnormal termination.

To test your knowledge of the above issues in ALGOL 60 and PL/I, you are asked to answer two simple questions about the programs given in the ALGOL 60 and PL/I quizzes.

(a)   Is the first print statement executed?

(b)   Is the last print statement executed?

Check the appropriate spaces. (Note: It is quite difficult to answer all questions correctly.)

ALGOL 60 QUIZ

1.   START: Yes ___ No ___   2.   START: Yes ___ No ___
      FINISH: Yes ___ No ___   FINISH: Yes ___ No ___

```
begin integer A,B,C;                begin integer A;
                                          boolean B;
    print ('START');
    A := 1;                             print ('START');
L:  B := 2;                             A := 1;
    goto L;                             B := A;
L:  C := 33;                            print ('FINISH');
    print ('FINISH');
                                    end
end
```


3.   START: Yes ___ No ___   4.   START: Yes ___ No ___
      FINISH: Yes ___ No ___   FINISH: Yes ___ No ___

```
begin real array A[1.3:1, 1.3:10];  begin procedure P(X,Y);
                                          X := Y+1;
    print ('START');                    integer A;
    A[4,2.6] := 1;
    print ('FINISH');                   print ('START');
                                        P(A,1);
end                                     print ('FINISH');

                                    end
```

5. START: Yes ___ No ___
    FINISH: Yes ___ No ___

```
begin procedure P(X,Y);
        X := Y+1;
      integer A;

      print ('START');
      P(A,true);
      print ('FINISH');

end
```

6. START: Yes ___ No ___
    FINISH: Yes ___ No ___

```
begin integer procedure P(F);
          integer procedure F;
          P := F(1,2,3);
        integer procedure A(X,Y);
          A := X+Y;

        print ('START');
        P(A);
        print ('FINISH');

end
```

7. START: Yes ___ No ___
    FINISH: Yes ___ No ___

```
begin procedure P(X);
          A := if B then X+1
                    else X(1);
        boolean B;
        integer A;

        print ('START');
        B := true;
        P(1);
        print ('FINISH');

end
```

8. START: Yes ___ No ___
    FINISH: Yes ___ No ___

```
begin procedure P(X);
          begin
          X := 1;
          if X then X := X(4,5);
          goto X;
          end;
        integer A;

        print ('START');
        P(A);
        print ('FINISH');

end
```

9. START: Yes ___ No ___
    FINISH: Yes ___ No ___

```
begin integer procedure G(F,N);
          integer procedure F;
          G := if N=0 then 1
                      else N*F(F,N-1);
        integer procedure FACT(N);
          FACT := G(G,N);
        integer I;

        print ('START');
        I := FACT(3);
        print ('FINISH');

end
```

PL/I QUIZ

1. START: Yes ___ No ___
    FINISH: Yes ___ No ___

```
P1:  PROCEDURE;
     DCL P1 PTR;

     PUT LIST ('START');
     P1 = NULL;
     PUT LIST ('FINISH');

END P1;
```

2. START: Yes ___ No ___
    FINISH: Yes ___ No ___

```
P2:  PROCEDURE;

         PUT LIST ('START');
         X = 0;
L:       DECLARE X FIXED;
         X = X + 3;
L:       X = X + 2;
         IF X<15 THEN GOTO L;
         PUT LIST ('FINISH');

     END P2;
```

3. START: Yes ___ No ___
    FINISH: Yes ___ No ___

```
P3:  PROCEDURE;
     DCL X STATIC;
     DCL 1 X, 2 A FIXED,
              2 B FLOAT,

     PUT LIST ('START');
     X.A = 1;
     X.B = 2.0;
     PUT LIST ('FINISH');

END P3;
```

4. START: Yes ___ No ___
    FINISH: Yes ___ No ___

```
P4:  PROCEDURE;
     DCL 1 A, 2 B, 3 I, 3 J;
     DCL B FIXED;

     PUT LIST ('START');
     B = 0;
     A.B.I = B;
     PUT LIST ('FINISH');

END P4;
```

5. START: Yes ___ No ___
    FINISH: Yes ___ No ___

```
P5:  PROCEDURE;
     DCL A PTR BASED(Q1);
     DCL B BASED(Q2);

     PUT LIST ('START');
     ALLOCATE B SET (A);
     B = 1;
     FREE A → B;
     PUT LIST ('FINISH');

END P5;
```

6. START: Yes ___ No ___
    FINISH: Yes ___ No ___

```
P6:  PROCEDURE;
     DCL A FIXED;

     PUT LIST ('START');
     A = 1;
     FREE A;
     PUT LIST ('FINISH');

END P6;
```

7. START: Yes ___ No ___
    FINISH: Yes ___ No ___

```
P7:  PROCEDURE;
     DCL (X DIRECT) FIXED;

     PUT LIST ('START');
     X = 5;
     X = SQRT(X**X + 1);
     PUT LIST ('FINISH');

END P7;
```

8. START: Yes ___ No ___
    FINISH: Yes ___ No ___

```
P8:  PROCEDURE;
     DCL X EXTERNAL INITIAL(6);

     PUT LIST ('START');
     X = SQRT (X**X + 1);
     PUT LIST ('FINISH');

END P8;
```

9. START: Yes ___ No ___
    FINISH: Yes ___ No ___

```
P9:  PROCEDURE;

     PUT LIST ('START');
     BEGIN;  DCL A CHAR(5) EXTERNAL;
         A = 'XXX';
     END;
     BEGIN;  DCL A PTR EXTERNAL;
         A = NULL;
     END;
     PUT LIST ('FINISH');

END P9;
```

CHAPTER THREE
TOP-DOWN PROGRAMMING

This chapter discusses in depth a technique of program development generally known as "top-down programming." The top-down approach presented here is based on the notions of "structured programming" (Refs. D1 and H1) and "stepwise refinement" (Ref. W4). While the technique is not a panacea for all programming ills, it does offer strong guidelines for an intelligent approach to a programming problem.

Top-down programming is an approach for developing computer programs in any programming language. Although one must be careful to avoid many pitfalls common to conventional techniques, the top-down approach is one of the major new developments in programming. The approach has the following characteristics:

1. *Exact Problem Definition:*
The programmer starts with an *exact* statement of the problem. It is senseless to start any program without a clear understanding of the problem.

2. *Initial Language Independence:*
The programmer initially uses expressions (often in English) that are relevant to the problem solution, even though the expressions cannot be directly transliterated into the target language. From statements that are *machine and language independent,* the programmer moves toward a final machine implementation in the target language.

3. *Design in Levels:*
The programmer designs the program in *levels*. At each level, the programmer considers alternative ways to refine some parts of the previous level. The programmer may look a level or two ahead to determine the best way to design the level at hand.

4. *Postponement of Details to Lower Levels:*
The programmer concentrates on critical broad issues at the initial levels, and

postpones details (for example, input/output headings, choice of identifiers, or data representation) until lower levels.

5. *Insuring Correctness at Each Level:*

After each level, the programmer rewrites the "program" as a correct formal statement. This step is critically important. He must *debug* his program and insure that all arguments to unwritten procedures or sections of code are explicit and correct, so that further sections of the program can be written *independently* without later changing the specifications or the interfaces between modules.

6. *Successive Refinements:*

Each level of the program is successively refined and debugged until the programmer obtains the completed program in the target language.

There are three notable characteristics of top-down programming. First, the overall problem must be clearly defined (see Proverb 1). Even if the original problem has been incompletely specified, it is senseless to start programming until there is a complete understanding of the problem that will allow the programmer to write the program without losing sight of the overall goal.

Second, at the upper levels the approach is machine- and language-independent. At this point the programmer is not constrained by any physical implementation (target machine or target language). He is writing the upper levels using a notation that is meaningful for the problem rather than for a machine.

The programmer's use of a particular notation involves no sacrifice: At each level the statements produced still represent a program in some sense. All that is lacking is the machine capable of executing the statements.

Third, at each level the programmer must "formalize" and "debug" the program so that further refinements will be absolutely correct with respect to previously designed levels. The importance of being complete and explicit at each level is by far the most misunderstood aspect of the top-down approach.

As for language independence, suppose that a programmer is working at an intermediate level and generates the following statements:

<u>if</u> the sum of the angles is 180°   <u>then</u> find the area of the triangle
                                                <u>else</u> find the area of the square

<u>print</u> area

The language of this statement is far removed from any contemporary computer language. On the other hand, the statement is perfectly clear to the programmer in that it reflects a section of code he wants to execute.

If indeed the sum of the angles is 180°, the area of the triangle is calculated and then this area is printed. If not, the area of the square is calculated and then this area is printed. The next refinement must spell out variables and procedures so that the final code will be correct.

The process of solving a problem using the top-down approach can be graphically represented by two trees. The first tree represents the top-down programming process as applied to a given problem. The second represents the actual structure of a *specific* program to solve the problem.

The first tree is shown in Fig. 3.1. The top-most level, P_0, represents the most general statement that can be made about the problem. Below this apex, the branches at each level of the tree represent the alternative design decisions for the programmer. The leaves of the tree represent all possible correct programs to solve the given problem. The top-down approach allows the programmer to make design decisions starting from the P_0 level and to follow the tree downwards with successive refinements towards a good solution. At each level the programmer examines the alternative branches and chooses the one that appears most suitable. However, if at any time the choice of any branch seems unwise, it is possible to backtrack up the tree one or more levels and select an alternative solution. The top-down process for a specific problem is a continuous path of design decisions from P_0 to a final program.

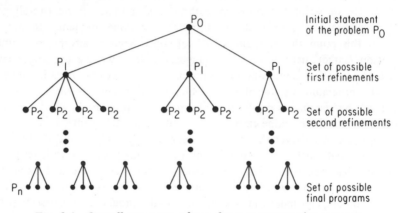

Fig. 3.1   Overall structure of top-down programming process

The second tree, illustrated in Fig. 3.2, represents the hierarchical structure of a *specific program* for which five levels were needed. Its top is again the most general statement of the problem. The nodes at each level are the components of the program at that level of refinement. At the bottom level, we end up with all the bits of code that make up the final program. The links between the levels represent the splitting of a block of code into subsections that are refinements of the given block. An example of such a completed tree is given at the end of the Kriegspiel example in this chapter.

There is, of course, a correspondence between the two trees. A given *level* on the tree of Fig. 3.2 corresponds to a *single node* on the same level in the tree of Fig. 3.1.

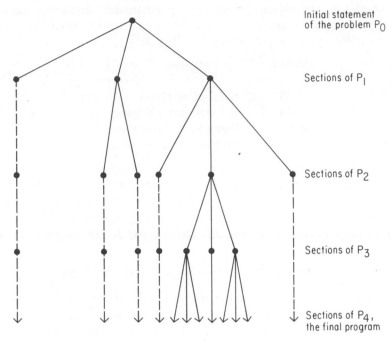

Initial statement
of the problem P_0

Sections of P_1

Sections of P_2

Sections of P_3

Sections of P_4,
the final program

Fig. 3.2   Top-down structure for a given program

The top-down approach is a programming technique that can be widely applied for consistently good results. While the technique is not an end in itself, it offers strong guidelines to the programmer. The rest of this chapter is devoted to two examples that illustrate precisely how the top-down method is used to write well-structured, modular programs. The examples also demonstrate that the method is by and large language-independent. The first example is a short and fairly simple problem, which is programmed in four languages. The second example is a more complex problem designed to illustrate the top-down approach in depth. The final main program is given in PL/I and ALGOL 60)

A PAYROLL PROBLEM

Mr. Nathan C. Ralston, President of P. Proverbs Institute, has just purchased a Universal Galactic 888 computer for his home office and 50,000 paycheck forms for his new computer. He turns over the first programming assignment, the payroll, to his chief programmer, Irene B. "Top-down" Malcolm. To complicate matters, Mr. Ralston is not to decide until next week which language will be the standard one for the Institute. So for the moment Irene is unable to choose a target language. As we shall see, this poses few problems.

Previously, the payroll was done by an independent data-processing company and only card input was supplied. These cards are to remain in use and have the following format (also indicated in Fig. 3.3):

Columns	Meaning
1-30	Name of employee
35-43	Social Security Number
45-48	Rate of pay (hourly wage)
51-54	Hours worked per week

The wage per hour and hours worked per week are input as four digit numbers with an implied medial decimal point; for example, an input of the four digits 3650 for hours worked is interpreted as 36.50 hours. For each employee input card, the program is to output a punched card containing the employee's name, social security number, and net pay. The net pay for an employee is to be determined by the rule:

$$NETPAY = GROSSPAY - TAXES - SS\_AMOUNT$$

where the tax rate is 4 percent and the social security rate is 1.75 percent of gross pay. Mr. Ralston makes one other request. He wants the weekly average number of hours worked per person printed on an additional last card.

<u>Input</u>: A sequence of employee work cards, each of which has the following data:

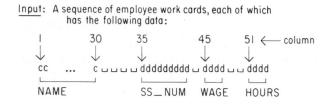

<u>Output</u>: A sequence of paychecks for each employee, of the form:

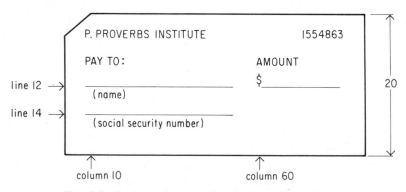

Fig. 3.3 Input and output for the payroll problem

At this point, Irene has a clear statement of the problem. Upon close analysis, she realizes that a number of error checks and other refinements should be made to the problem definition. However, because of the time constraints, she decides to follow instructions exactly to construct her solution. First, at the topmost level, she states the problem:

$$P_0$$

```
Process the Payroll Cards
```

Irene next considers the overall structure of the program. She must determine the basic order of the calculations and the condition under which the program terminates. After some deliberation, she obtains P_1, as shown:

$$P_1$$

```
    Initialize tor program

A:  read the next employee card

    if no more data

            then calculate and print average hours worked
                 stop

            else process the card and check
                 update for weekly average
                 go back to (A) for next employee
```

Note that P_1 is a more refined statement of the problem and is described basically in English.

Irene next formalizes the calculations to isolate exactly the variables used in each piece of code. This practice insures that the interfaces for each piece of code will be spelled out *before* proceeding further. Since the calculations are fairly simple, Irene can write them down directly. She *deliberately* avoids input/output for the moment. It is one of the details she postpones until the overall structure of the program is correct. The result is P_2, as shown:

$$P_2$$

```
    /* Initialize for program */

    TAXRATE       = 0.04
    SS RATE       = 0.0175
    TOTAL_HOURS   = 0.0
    NOS_EMPLOYEES = 0

    /* read next employee card */
A:  read CARD into (NAME, SS_NUM, WAGE, HOURS)
```

```
if no more data

then /* calculate and print average, and stop */
        AVERAGE = TOTAL_HOURS / NOS_EMPLOYEES
        print (AVERAGE) on check stub
        stop;

else /* process the card and check */
        GROSS_PAY = WAGE*HOURS
        NET_PAY   = GROSS_PAY - GROSS_PAY*TAXRATE - GROSS_PAY*SS_RATE
        print (NAME, NET_PAY, SS_NUM) on check stub

    /* update for weekly average */
        TOTAL_HOURS   = TOTAL_HOURS + HOURS
        NOS_EMPLOYEES = NOS_EMPLOYEES + 1

    /* repeat for next employee */
        goto A
```

It is important to note that although P_1 and P_2 are not programs in any existing language, it is perfectly sound to make sure that there are no errors even at these levels. "Debugging" at each intermediate level in the top-down approach is *critical.* For example, suppose Irene omitted from P_2 the line,

$$\text{TOTAL\_HOURS} = \text{TOTAL\_HOURS} + \text{HOURS}$$

This omission causes the line

$$\text{AVERAGE} = \text{TOTAL\_HOURS} / \text{NOS\_EMPLOYEES}$$

to give a value of 0 for AVERAGE, a clearly incorrect result. If an error like this is made, it should be detected at this level, *not* in the final program.

Now Irene turns to I/O. First, how will she determine "no more data"? As a flag for "no more data," she decides to insert a card punched with nines in columns 45-48 at the end of the input deck. When the read statement labeled A is executed, the WAGE will be 99.99, and a test for the condition can be included. Based on the pay check form, Irene specifies the I/O formats and obtains P_3. Note that in format statements, the numbers in parentheses represent column positions.

$$P_3$$

```
/* Initialize for program */

    CARDS:  format [NAME(1-30), SS_NUM(35-43), WAGE(45-48), HOURS(51-54)]
    CHECK:  format [line 12, NAME(10-39), NET_PAY(61-66), line 14, SS_NUM(10-18)]
    LAST:   format [line 12, 'AVERAGE IS'(10-19), AVERAGE(21-25)]

    TAXRATE       = 0.04
    SS_RATE       = 0.0175
    TOTAL_HOURS   = 0.0
    NOS_EMPLOYEES = 0
```

```
/* Read next employee card */
   A:   read   CARD   into(NAME,SS_NUM,WAGE,HOURS) using CARDS format

/* More data ? */
   if WAGE = 99.99

        then /* calculate and print average, and stop */
                AVERAGE = TOTAL_HOURS / NOS_EMPLOYEES
                print (AVERAGE) using LAST format
                stop

        else /* process the card and check */
                GROSS_PAY = WAGE*HOURS
                NET_PAY   = GROSS_PAY - GROSS_PAY*TAXRATE - GROSS_PAY*SS_RATE
                print (NAME,NET_PAY,SS_NUM) using CHECK format

        /* update for weekly average */
                TOTAL_HOURS   = TOTAL_HOURS + HOURS
                NOS_EMPLOYEES = NOS_EMPLOYEES + 1

        /* repeat for next employee */
                goto A
```

And *voila!* Irene has a correct "program"! All that is left is to determine the final language. But luck is against our programmer. Mr Ralston informs Irene that the decision on the standard language will not be made until Friday morning, and the payroll must be out Friday afternoon. Irene decides to map out the solution in four languages: FORTRAN IV, PL/I, BASIC, and COBOL (Examples 3.1, 3.2, 3.3, and 3.4). She hopes to be prepared whatever comes on Friday. We wish her luck!

Perhaps it would be wise at this point to compare briefly the advantages and disadvantages of each of the four languages with respect to the payroll problem. (Remember Proverb 25, "Consider Another Language"?)

In the FORTRAN program the format statements are concise but somewhat difficult to read. The lack of more powerful control structures and better facilities for handling strings are clear debits.

In the PL/I program, the format statements are also difficult to read. Although PL/I has stronger control structures and better string facilities, the advantages over FORTRAN are significant but not overwhelming.

The BASIC program, although short, is somewhat more opaque. The lack of lengthy identifiers is a strong debit, and the output statements are hard to write mainly because of the need to type out blank spaces.

The COBOL program is quite long-winded, the usual case in COBOL. Even though the "format" statements are long, they are quite manageable and easy to change. The arithmetic facility in COBOL is quite annoying for those used to FORTRAN or PL/I.

All in all, we give the edge to the PL/I program, with the FORTRAN program being a close second. But, of course, readers are more than welcome to make their own comparisons.

Example 3.1 PL/I Payroll Program

$$P_4$$

```
PAYROLL:  PROCEDURE OPTIONS(MAIN);

     /* PAYROLL FOR P. PROVERBS INSTITUTE, BY I.B. MALCOLM */

     /* INITIALIZE FOR PROGRAM */
     DECLARE (INFILE INPUT, OUTFILE OUTPUT) FILE,
             NAME CHARACTERS(30), SSNUM CHARACTER(9),
             (AVERAGE, HOURS, WAGE, NET_PAY, GROSS_PAY, TAXRATE, SS_RATE
             TOTAL_HOURS, NOS_EMPLOYEES)  FIXED DECIMAL(8,4);

     CARDS: FORMAT (A(30), X(4), A(9), X(1), F(4,2), X(2), F(4,2));
     CHECK: FORMAT (SKIP(12), COLUMN(10), A, COLUMN(61), F(7,2), SKIP(2),
                    COLUMN(10), A, SKIP(6));
     LAST:  FORMAT (SKIP(11), COLUMN(10), A, F(5,2));

     TAXRATE       = 0.04
     SS_RATE       = 0.0175
     TOTAL_HOURS   = 0.0
     NOS_EMPLOYEES = 0

     /* IF NO MORE DATA THEN CALCULATE AND PRINT AVERAGE, AND STOP */
     /* IN PL/I WE DO NOT NEED THE SPECIAL LAST CARD */
        ON ENDFILE(INFILE)
        BEGIN;
           AVERAGE = TOTAL_HOURS / NOS_EMPLOYEES;
           PUT FILE(OUTFILE) EDIT('AVERAGE IS', AVERAGE)  (R(LAST));
           STOP;
        END;

     /* READ NEXT EMPLOYEE CARD */
     A:   GET FILE(INFILE) EDIT(NAME,SSNUM,WAGE,HOURS)  (R(CARDS));

        /* PROCESS THE CARD AND CHECK */
           GROSS_PAY = WAGE*HOURS;
           NET_PAY   = GROSS_PAY - GROSS_PAY*TAXRATE - GROSS_PAY*SS_RATE;
           PUT FILE(OUTFILE) EDIT(NAME, NET_PAY,SSNUM)  (R(CHECK));

        /* UPDATE FOR WEEKLY AVERAGE */
           TOTAL_HOURS   = TOTAL_HOURS + HOURS;
           NOS_EMPLOYEES = NOS_EMPLOYEES + 1;

        /* REPEAT FOR NEXT EMPLOYEE */
           GOTO A;

END PAYROLL;
```

Example 3.2   Fortran IV Payroll Program

$$P_4$$

```
C      /* PAYROLL FOR P. PROVERBS INSTITUTE, BY I.B. MALCOLM */
C
C      /* MAXIMUM LENGTH STRING VALUE FOR VARIABLES IS
C          4 TO 8 CHARACTERS, DEPENDING ON MACHINE.   HERE WE
C          ASSUME IT IS 6, AND TREAT NAME AND SSNUM AS ARRAYS */
C
C      /* INITIALIZE FOR PROGRAM */
       INTEGER CARD, PRINTR, SSNUM
       REAL   NETPAY
       DIMENSION  NAME(5), SSNUM(2)
       DATA  CARD, PRINTR /5,6/
C
   100 FORMAT (5A6, 4X, 1A6, 1A3, 1X, F4.2, 2X, F4.2)
   200 FORMAT (11(/), 1X, 9X, 5A6, 21X, F7.2 // 1X, 9X, 1A6, 1A3, 7(/))
   300 FORMAT (11(/), 1X , 9X, 11HAVERAGE IS , F5.2)
C
C
C
       TXRATE = 0.04
       SSRATE = 0.0175
       TOTHRS = 0.0
       NOEMPL = 0
C
C
C      /* READ NEXT EMPLOYEE CARD */
    10 READ(CARD,100) NAME, SSNUM, WAGE, HOURS
C
C      /* IF NO MORE DATA, CALCULATE AND PRINT AVERAGE, AND STOP */
       IF (WAGE .NE. 99.99) GOTO 20
           AVERAG = TOTHRS / FLOAT(NOEMPL)
           WRITE(PRINTR,300) AVERAG
           STOP
C
C      /* ELSE PROCESS THE CARD AND CHECK */
    20     GRPAY = WAGE*HOURS
           NETPAY = GRPAY - GRPAY*TXRATE - GRPAY*SSRATE
           WRITE(PRINTR,200) NAME, NETPAY, SSNUM
C
C      /* UPDATE FOR WEEKLY AVERAGE */
           TOTHRS = TOTHRS + HOURS
           NOEMPL = NOEMPL + 1
C
C      /* REPEAT FOR NEXT EMPLOYEE */
           GOTO 10
C
       END
```

Example 3.3   BASIC Payroll Program

$$P_4$$

```
10    REM  /* PAYROLL FOR P. PROVERBS INSTITUTE, BY I.B. MALCOLM */
20    REM
30    REM  /* INITIALIZE FOR PROGRAM */
40    REM  /* MAP OF IDENTIFIERS */
50    REM       T1 = TAXRATE, S1 = SS_RATE, N$ = NAME, W = WAGE
60    REM       H = HOURS, T = TOTAL_HOURS, P = NET_PAY, G = GROSS_PAY
70    REM       A = AVERAGE, N = NOS_EMPLOYEES, S$ = SS_NUM
80    REM
90    REM  /* BASIC HAS NO EXPLICIT FORMAT STATEMENT */
100            LET T1 = 0.04
110            LET S1 = 0.0175
120            LET T = 0.0
130            LET N = 0
140   REM
200   REM  /* READ NEXT EMPLOYEE CARD */
210            INPUT N$, S$, W, H
300   REM
310   REM  /* IF NO MORE DATA, CALCULATE AND PRINT AVERAGE, AND STOP */
320            IF W < >99.99 THEN 420.
330               LET A = T/N
340               FOR I = 1 TO 11
350                  PRINT
360               NEXT I
370               PRINT "          AVERAGE IS ";    A
380               STOP
400   REM
410   REM
420   REM  /* PROCESS THE CARD */
430            LET G = W*H
440            LET P = ( - G*T1 - G*S1
500   REM  /* PRINT CHECK */
510            FOR I = 1 TO 11
520               PRINT
530            NEXT I
540            PRINT "          "; N$; "                    "; P
550            PRINT
560            PRINT "          "; S$
570            FOR I = 1 TO 6
580               PRINT
590            NEXT I
600   REM
610   REM  /* UPDATE FOR WEEKLY AVERAGE */
620            LET T = T + H
630            LET N = N + 1
640   REM
650   REM  /* REPEAT FOR NEXT EMPLOYEE */
660            GOTO 210
700   END
```

Example 3.4   COBOL Payroll Program

$$P_4$$

IDENTIFICATION DIVISION.

PROGRAM-ID. PAYROLL.
AUTHOR. I B MALCOLM.
INSTALLATION. P PROVERBS INSTITUTE.
DATE-WRITTEN. 1/1/74.
DATE-COMPILED. 1/7/74.

REMARKS. THE COBOL IDENTIFICATION AND ENVIRONMENT DIVISIONS HAVE NO
         ANALOG IN THE OTHER LANGUAGES: THE DATA DIVISION CORRESPONDS
         TO THE DECLARATION AND INITIALIZATION OF VARIABLES: THE FILE
         DESCRIPTION (FD) FOR CARD-FILE CORRESPONDS TO THE CARD FORMAT
         (100), THE FD FOR CHECK-FILE CORRESPONDS TO THE CHECK FORMAT
         (200) AND AVERAGE LINE FORMAT: ALSO NOTE THAT COBOL DOESN'T
         NEED THE SPECIAL LAST CARD BECAUSE IT TESTS DIRECTLY FOR THE
         END OF FILE.

ENVIRONMENT DIVISION.

CONFIGURATION SECTION.
     SOURCE-COMPUTER. UNIVERSAL GALACTIC 888.
     OBJECT-COMPUTER. UNIVERSAL GALACTIC 888.

INPUT-OUTPUT SECTION.
FILE CONTROL.
     SELECT CARD-FILE ASSIGN TO CARD-READER.
     SELECT CHECK-FILE ASSIGN TO PRINTER.

DATA DIVISION.

FILE SECTION.

FD   CARD-FILE DATA RECORD IS CARD.
01   CARD.
     02 NAME PICTURE IS X(30),
     02 FILLER PICTURE IS X(4).
     02 SS-NUM PICTURE IS 9(9).
     02 FILLER PICTURE IS X.
     02 WAGE PICTURE IS 99V99.
     02 FILLER PICTURE IS X(2).
     02 HOURS PICTURE IS 99V99.
     02 FILLER PICTURE IS X(18).

FD   CHECK-FILE DATA RECORDS ARE
         CHECK-LINE-12 CHECK-LINE-14 AVERAGE-LINE, BLANK-LINE.
01   CHECK-LINE-12.
     02 FILLER PICTURE IS X(9).
     02 NAME PICTURE IS X(30).
     02 FILLER PICTURE IS X(21).
     02 NET-PAY PICTURE IS ***9.99.
     02 FILLER PICTURE IS X(5).

Example 3.4   COBOL Payroll Program (cont'd)

```
01  CHECK-LINE-14.
    02 FILLER PICTURE IS X(9).
    02 SS-NUM PICTURE IS 9(9).
    02 FILLER PICTURE IS X(54).

01  AVERAGE-LINE.
    02 FILLER PICTURE IS X(9).
    02 AVERAGE-IS PICTURE IS X(11).
    02 AVERAGE PICTURE IS 99.99.
    02 FILLER PICTURE IS X(47).

01  BLANK-LINE PICTURE IS X(72).

WORKING-STORAGE SECTION.

77  TOTAL-HOURS PICTURE IS 9999V99  VALUE IS ZERO.
77  NOS-EMPLOYEES PICTURE IS 999 VALUE IS ZERO.
77  GROSS-PAY PICTURE IS 999V99.
77  TAXRATE PICTURE IS V99 VALUE IS .04.
77  SS-RATE PICTURE IS V9999 VALUE IS .0175.

PROCEDURE DIVISION.
HOUSEKEEPING.

    OPEN INPUT CARD-FILE OUTPUT CHECK-FILE.
    MOVE SPACES TO CHECK-LINE-12 CHECK-LINE-14 AVERAGE-LINE.
    MOVE SPACES TO BLANK-LINE.
A.  READ CARD-FILE RECORD AT END PERFORM WRAPUP.
    GO TO PROCESS-CARD.

WRAPUP.

    DIVIDE NOS-EMPLOYEES INTO TOTAL-HOURS GIVING AVERAGE ROUNDED.
    MOVE 'AVERAGE IS ' TO AVERAGE-IS.
    WRITE AVERAGE-LINE AFTER ADVANCING 12 LINES.
    CLOSE CARD-FILE CHECK-FILE.
    STOP RUN.

PROCESS-CARD.
    MULTIPLY HOURS BY WAGE GIVING GROSS-PAY ROUNDED.
    COMPUTE NET-PAY ROUNDED = GROSS-PAY - GROSS-PAY * TAXRATE -
        GROSS-PAY * SS-RATE.

PRINT-CHECK.
    MOVE CORRESPONDING CARD TO CHECK-LINE-12 CHECK-LINE-14.
    WRITE CHECK-LINE-12 AFTER ADVANCING 12 LINES.
    WRITE CHECK-LINE-14 AFTER ADVANCING 2 LINES.
    WRITE BLANK-LINE AFTER ADVANCING 6 LINES.

UPDATE.
    ADD HOURS TO TOTAL-HOURS.
    ADD 1 TO NOS-EMPLOYEES.

REPEAT-FOR-NEXT-EMPLOYEE.
    GO TO A.
```

KRIEGSPIEL CHECKERS

Bob and Bill started playing checkers early in their youth. Upon entering the Army they brought along their checker boards and continued playing. One day in communications school, they met Jasper Cromwell. Jasper was a rather mediocre player, but he introduced Bob and Bill to an interesting variant of the game called "Kriegspiel." In Kriegspiel checkers the players sit in isolated areas, each having a separate board containing only his own pieces. As each player proposes a move, a third person, the referee, tells the player that: (a) The proposed move is legal, and the opponent will be directed to move; (b) the proposed move is illegal, and the player must propose another move, or (c) the proposed move wins and the game is over. (Note: For readers who play checkers, the Kriegspiel variant will be much more interesting than it first appears.)

Bob and Bill were fascinated, but every game took so long that they modified the game slightly by adding the following rules: (a) In addition to winning a game by capturing or blocking all of his opponent's pieces, a player also wins by getting the first king. (b) When a player proposes a jump that is legal but only part of a multiple jump, the referee informs him: "Further jump required—enter next square." The player then continues to propose further jumps until the multiple jump is completed. With these changes, Bob and Bill launched into a series of games with Jasper acting as referee.

But all good things come to an end. The Pentagon computer, knowing nothing of the tournament, issued orders assigning Bob to Alaska, Bill to Iceland, and Jasper to the Computer Center in Fort Lauderdale, Florida. Bob and Bill lost no time re-establishing communications with Jasper. However, Jasper now found himself without the time to referee. One day, while dusting off the computers, Jasper suddenly realized a solution. Why not let a computer do the work? Being a competent programmer, trained, of course, at the Programming Proverbs Institute, he started work immediately, using the top-down approach.

Let us pause here to be sure we understand Jasper's problem. (Remember? Define the problem completely!) Jasper needs a program that can process a sequence of moves and monitor the game. Hence the program must "know" the rules of checkers, that is, insure that black always moves first, insist that a jump be made when one is possible, verify the legality of moves, determine when the game is over, and so forth.

Furthermore, the program must accept moves in a format familiar to the players. In this case, a move consists of two numbers corresponding to squares on the standard checkerboard, as illustrated in Fig. 3.4. The first number is the original square of the moving piece, and the second number is its destination square. The program must also output "messages" based on whether the proposed move is legal or nonlegal, requires a jump continuation, or terminates the game.

The Outer Structure of the Program

Jasper begins with a general statement of the problem:

$$P_0$$

```
Monitor the Game of Kriegspiel Checkers
```

Excellent! If nothing else, Jasper knows what the problem is. After some deliberation, he splits the problem into four sections, as shown in P_1.

$$P_1$$

```
          initialize for program;

A:        input a proposed move;

          if move is legal
             then process the move;
             else repeat (A);

          if the game is over
             then end the game;
             else change players
                  and repeat (A);
```

Now that the overall logical structure has been determined, Jasper's next refinement is to rewrite the program (in its present form) so that all *interactions* between sections of the code are clearly spelled out. The legality of a proposed move is dependent upon the MOVE, the PLAYER who proposed it, and the BOARD. The end of the game occurs when there *is* a *king* on the BOARD for the PLAYER, or when there is *no* possible *move* on the BOARD for the OPPONENT.

These and other sections of the code are formalized as procedure calls with appropriate arguments. The result is P_2. (Note: There is a slight error in P_2. Can you find it and completely debug this level before reading on?)

$$P_2$$

```
          INITIALIZE (BOARD,PLAYER);

A:        input (MOVE);

          if LEGAL_MOVE(BOARD,MOVE,PLAYER)

              then print('LEGAL MOVE');
                   UPDATE_BOARD (BOARD,MOVE,PLAYER);

              else print('ILLEGAL MOVE, TRY AGAIN');
                   goto A;
```

```
if IS_KING(BOARD) or NO_MOVE(BOARD,OPPONENT)
   then print('WINNER IS', PLAYER);
        stop;
   else PLAYER = OPPONENT;
        goto A;
```

The newly formalized sections of code require definitions, but these definitions are quite clear at this point and can be "programmed" later, after other critical design decisions have been made.

Jasper continues by making some refinements of P_2. Passing BOARD as a parameter to every procedure is somewhat inefficient, and the uses of the BOARD variable are obvious. For efficiency and clarity, Jasper decides that BOARD should not be passed as an explicit argument to each procedure. Hence, BOARD will be made a global variable and dropped from the argument lists. Next, a single-valued identifier MOVE is not adequate to represent a proposed move. Since a move consists of two squares from Fig. 3.4, Jasper elects to have two variables (SQ1 and SQ2) represent a move. Jasper now notices a slight error in P_2 (mentioned earlier). He has used OPPONENT freely but has never given it a value. Obviously, the OPPONENT is the OTHER(PLAYER), and for the moment he inserts this new function call.

Jasper *deliberately* postpones decisions about data representations of the board and players. Such decisions are usually limiting because there is a tendency to program around the properties of the representation. With these considerations, he obtains P_3. Cautioned by the unobserved bug in P_2, Jasper carefully checks P_3 at this point to ensure correctness.

$$P_3$$

```
     INITIALIZE(BOARD, PLAYER);

A:   input(SQ1,SQ2);

     if LEGAL_MOVE(SQ1,SQ2,PLAYER)

        then print('LEGAL MOVE');
             UPDATE_BOARD(SQ1,SQ2,PLAYER);

        else print('ILLEGAL MOVE, TRY AGAIN');
             goto A;

     OPPONENT = OTHER(PLAYER);

     if IS_KING( ) or NO_MOVE(OPPONENT)
        then print('WINNER IS', PLAYER);
             stop;
        else PLAYER = OPPONENT;
             goto A;
```

Since the design decisions regarding game termination have all been made in P_3, Jasper turns to the other sections of the program. Rather than write the complicated function LEGAL_MOVE separately, he decides to break down the legality test and its consequences into smaller parts. This decision is typical of the top-down process because it reduces the problem to smaller and simpler procedure modules.

The rules of checkers state that a player must jump if a jump exists. Looking a level or two ahead, Jasper sees that sweeping the board for possible jumps is a lengthy process. If the proposed move is a jump, the sweep can be eliminated. Therefore, he first checks to see if the input move is a legal jump. Since a jump might be the first part of a multiple jump, the program must immediately check if the player making a jump CAN_JUMP again. If the player can, then a special subroutine must be invoked to CONTINUE_THE_JUMP.

Jasper has now taken care of jumps. If the proposed move is not a jump, then the move must be checked to see if it is a LEGAL_NON_JUMP, and the sweep to check that NO_JUMP_EXISTS must be verified. If both checks hold, then the player has input a legal move. Otherwise, the proposed move is illegal and an alternate move must be requested. With these considerations Jasper now makes a major refinement to obtain P_4.

$$P_4$$

```
        INITIALIZE (BOARD, PLAYER);

A:      input(SQ1,SQ2);

        if LEGAL_JUMP(SQ1,SQ2,PLAYER)

            then print('LEGAL MOVE');
                 UPDATE_BOARD(SQ1,SQ2,PLAYER);

                 if CAN_JUMP(SQ2,PLAYER)
                    then CONTINUE_THE_JUMP(SQ2,PLAYER);

            else if LEGAL_NON_JUMP(SQ1,SQ2,PLAYER) and
                    NO_JUMP_EXISTS(PLAYER)
                    then print('LEGAL MOVE');
                         UPDATE_BOARD(SQ1,SQ2,PLAYER);
                    else print('ILLEGAL MOVE, TRY AGAIN');
                         goto A;

        OPPONENT = OTHER(PLAYER);

        is IS_KING( ) or NO_MOVE(OPPONENT)
           then print('WINNER IS', PLAYER);
                stop;
           else PLAYER = OPPONENT;
                goto A;
```

P_4 stands alone. Jasper carefully debugs P_4 to insure that it is indeed correct. He determines that it does indeed handle all contingencies of the stated problem. What remains is for Jasper to specify what each procedure in the program does.

Data Representation

Before Jasper can proceed, he must determine the "specific structure of his data representations." This six-dollar phrase means that Jasper must figure out a way to represent the checkerboard and the player's pieces in his program. Remember that Bob and Bill have only the standard checkerboard (Fig. 3.4). There is a great temptation to code the standard checkerboard numbering system directly into his program, but Jasper finds that this is more difficult than it appears.

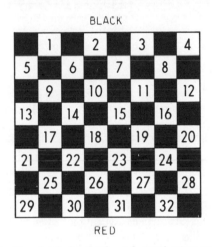

BLACK

RED

Fig. 3.4 Standard checkerboard numbering system

First, look at square 10 of Fig. 3.4. A black piece on that square can make a nonjump move to 14 or 15. So the possible moves are 10 + 4 = 14, and 10 + 5 = 15, or simply, +4 and +5. But from square 15 the black moves are to squares 18 and 19, or simply +3 and +4. A similar situation exists for red, except that the moves are −3, −4 and −4, −5, since the move direction is reversed. Jasper could sort out which moves use the 4,5 rule and which moves use the 3,4 rule, but another problem remains. Black's first row (squares 1 through 4) uses the +4, +5 rule. But what about square 4? Using the +4,+5 rule, 8 is a legal square, but 9 is not.

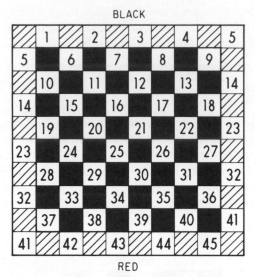

Fig. 3.5 Samuel's board numbering for internal representation

To avoid these difficulties, Jasper looks for an alternative. Being well read, he chooses an ingenious representation for the checkerboard devised by A.L. Samuel (Ref. S1), which is shown in Fig. 3.5.

Notice that regardless of the square, the possible directed moves for black are always +4 and +5, and for red, −4 and −5. The added border squares are "flag" squares. They will contain some value to indicate that they do not represent legal squares. When a proposed move goes from a legal square to a "flag" square, the move can be quickly detected as illegal. Notice also that opposite border squares are labeled with the same numbers. This causes no problem since they are flag squares and need not have distinct numbers.

Although this representation solves many problems, it has one inconvenience. Bob and Bill are using the standard checkerboard (Fig. 3.4), whereas the program uses that of Fig. 3.5. This inconsistency means that input moves will have to be converted to Jasper's representation. Jasper thus provides a conversion routine called OBTAIN to input proposed moves and convert them to their internal representation.

Jasper now has a board. But what is he going to put on it? Checkers? Yes, in a sense, but he will have to create a representation for them. He decides to represent BLACK pieces by the number +1, RED pieces by the number −1, VACANT squares by the number 0, and the additional border squares by the number 2. The initial board configuration is shown in Fig. 3.6. The representation of BLACK and RED by +1 and −1 has two distinct (perhaps tricky) advantages. The OPPONENT is simply −PLAYER, and the sign (plus or minus) of the direction of a move is the same as that of the PLAYER.

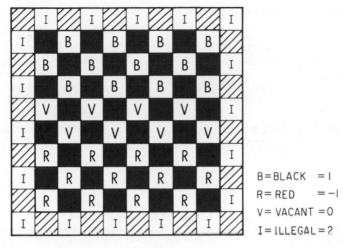

Fig. 3.6 Status of board at start of game.

With these design decisions, Jasper can now write P_5, the complete main "program."

$$P_5$$

```
/* INITIALIZE FOR PROGRAM */

array BOARD subscripts [1] to [45];
BLACK   = 1;
RED     = -1;
VACANT  = 0;
ILLEGAL = 2;
PLAYER  = BLACK;
INITIALIZE (BOARD);


/* MAIN WORKING PROGRAM */

A: OBTAIN (SQ1,SQ2);

    if LEGAL_JUMP(SQ1,SQ2,PLAYER)

        then print ('LEGAL MOVE');
             UPDATE_BOARD (SQ1,SQ2,PLAYER);

             if CAN_JUMP (SQ2,PLAYER)
                then CONTINUE_THE_JUMP (SQ2,PLAYER);

        else if LEGAL_NON_JUMP(SQ1,SQ2,PLAYER) and
                NO_JUMP_EXISTS(PLAYER)
             then print('LEGAL MOVE');
                  UPDATE_BOARD(SQ1,SQ2,PLAYER);
             else print ('ILLEGAL MOVE, TRY AGAIN');
                  goto A:
```

```
OPPONENT = -PLAYER;


if IS_KING( ) or NO_MOVE(OPPONENT)
   then print('THE WINNER IS', PLAYER);
        stop;
   else PLAYER = OPPONENT;
        goto A;
```

While P_5 is given in Jasper's own notation, he can now easily transform P_5 into P_6 for both ALGOL 60 and PL/I. These main programs are shown as Examples 3.5 and 3.6.

Example 3.5 P_6 —ALGOL 60 Kriegspiel Main Program

```
begin  KRIEGSPIEL;

   comment /* Initialize for program */ ;

   integer BLACK, RED, VACANT, ILLEGAL, PLAYER, OPPONENT, SQ1, SQ2;
   integer array BOARD[1:45];

   comment /* The remaining procedure declarations can be placed here */ ;

   BLACK   := 1;
   RED     := -1;
   VACANT  := 0;
   ILLEGAL := 2;
   PLAYER  := BLACK;
   INITIALIZE(BOARD);


A: OBTAIN(SQ1,SQ2);

   if LEGALJUMP(SQ1,SQ2,PLAYER)

      then begin print ('LEGAL MOVE');
                  UPDATEBOARD (SQ1,SQ2,PLAYER);

                  if CANJUMP(SQ2,PLAYER)
                     then CONTINUETHEJUMP(SQ2,PLAYER);
           end

      else if LEGALNONJUMP(SQ1,SQ2,PLAYER) ∧
              NOJUMPEXISTS(PLAYER)
           then begin print ('LEGAL MOVE');
                       UPDATEBOARD (SQ1,SQ2,PLAYER);
                end
           else begin print ('ILLEGAL MOVE, TRY AGAIN');
                       goto A;
                end;

   OPPONENT := -PLAYER;

   if ISKING( ) ∨ NOMOVE(OPPONENT)
```

```
            then begin print ('THE WINNER IS', PLAYER);
                        stop;
                  end
            else begin PLAYER := OPPONENT;
                        print ('CHANGE PLAYER TO', PLAYER);
                        goto A;
                  end;

end KRIEGSPIEL;
```

Example 3.6   P₆—PL/I Kriegspiel Main Program

```
KRIEGSPIEL:  PROCEDURE  OPTIONS(MAIN);

   /*  INITIALIZE FOR PROGRAM */

   DECLARE (BLACK,RED,VACANT,ILLEGAL,PLAYER,OPPONENT,SQ1,SQ2)  FIXED;
   DECLARE  BOARD(1,45)  FIXED;

   /* DECLARATIONS FOR TWO GLOBAL VARIABLES SIMULATING TRUE AND FALSE */
   DECLARE  (TRUE, FALSE)  BIT(1) INITIAL('1'B, '0'B);

   /* THE REMAINING PROCEDURE DECLARATIONS MAY BE PLACED HERE */

   BLACK   = 1;
   RED     = -1;
   VACANT  = 0;
   ILLEGAL = 2;
   PLAYER  = BLACK;
   CALL INITIALIZE(BOARD) ;


   /* MAIN WORKING PROGRAM */

A: CALL OBTAIN (SQ1,SQ2);

   IF LEGAL_JUMP(SQ1,SQ2,PLAYER)

      THEN BEGIN;
              PUT LIST ('LEGAL MOVE');
              CALL UPDATE_BOARD(SQ1,SQ2,PLAYER);

              IF CAN_JUMP(SQ2,PLAYER)
                 THEN CALL CONTINUE_THE_JUMP (SQ2,PLAYER);
           END;

      ELSE IF LEGAL_NON_JUMP(SQ1,SQ2,PLAYER) & NO_JUMP_EXISTS(PLAYER)
              THEN BEGIN;
                      PUT LIST ('LEGAL MOVE');
                      CALL UPDATE_BOARD (SQ1,SQ2,PLAYER);
                   END;
              ELSE BEGIN;
                      PUT LIST ('ILLEGAL MOVE, TRY AGAIN');
                      GOTO A;
                   END;

   OPPONENT = -PLAYER;
```

Example 3.6 P₆—PL/I Kriegspiel Main Program (cont'd)

```
IF IS_KING( ) | NO_MOVE(OPPONENT)
    THEN BEGIN;  PUT LIST ('THE WINNER IS', PLAYER);
                 STOP;
         END;
    ELSE BEGIN;  PLAYER = OPPONENT;
                 PRINT LIST('CHANGE PLAYER TO', PLAYER);
                 GOTO A;
         END;
END KRIEGSPIEL;
```

The Remaining Procedures

Now Jasper can begin the task of specifying each procedure. Since they are quite straightforward, we will not elaborate on each. We will describe one procedure to give the reader a feel for operating on the board.

One important point must be made. Using the top-down approach, the main program has been so carefully defined and structured that all the procedures can now be written *independently*. Any procedures that fit their required definitions for the main program will now suffice.

As the sample procedure, we choose LEGAL_JUMP. The procedure takes three arguments, SQ1, SQ2, and PLAYER. It returns the value *true* if the PLAYER has a legal jump from SQ1 to SQ2, and *false* otherwise. For a legal jump, the following conditions must be met:

(1)   The moving player must have a piece on SQ1.
(2)   SQ2 must be vacant.
(3)   SQ2 must equal SQ1±8 (or SQ1±10).
(4)   The intervening square, SQ1±4 (or SQ1±5) must contain an opponent's piece.

The sign, + or −, depends on the moving player, black or red. Since black is represented by +1 and red by −1, the sign S can be set to the value of PLAYER. The complete LEGAL_JUMP procedure is given on page 88 both in PL/I and ALGOL 60.

The complete, final program comprises the main program and the declaration of all procedures. These procedures are given in Example 3.7 in ALGOL 60; the corresponding PL/I procedures are left as an exercise.

The reader should go over the main program and subprograms to satisfy himself that they work correctly. A completed tree representing the hierarchical-structure for this program is illustrated in Fig. 3.7. (Final note: The reader may have observed several ways of "speeding up" the Kriegspiel program. Efficiency was not at all a major design criterion in our development, although it could have been. Can you propose several changes to make the program more efficient?)

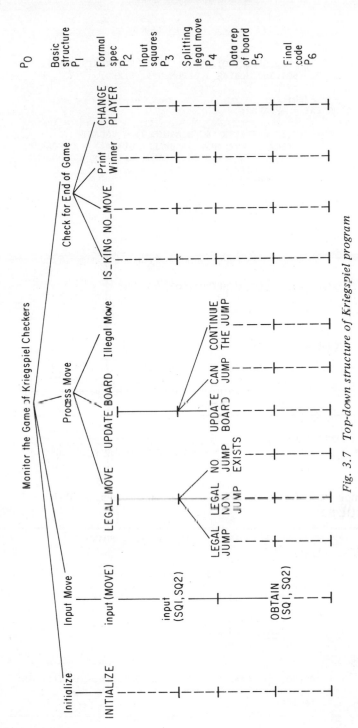

Fig. 3.7 Top-down structure of Kriegspiel program

<u>PL/I   LEGAL JUMP PROCEDURE</u>

```
LEGAL_JUMP:  PROCEDURE(SQ1,SQ2,PLAYER)  RETURNS(BIT(1));
    DECLARE (SQ1,SQ2,PLAYER,S,OPPONENT)  FIXED;

    S = PLAYER;
    OPPONENT = -PLAYER;

    IF BOARD(SQ1) = PLAYER  &  BOARD(SQ2) = VACANT    &
            ( (SQ2 = SQ1+S*8   &  BOARD(SQ1+S*4) = OPPONENT) |
              (SQ2 = SQ1+S*10  &  BOARD(SQ1+S*5) = OPPONENT) )
        THEN RETURN(TRUE);
        ELSE RETURN(FALSE);

END LEGAL_JUMP;
```

<u>ALGOL 60 LEGAL JUMP PROCEDURE</u>

```
boolean procedure   LEGALJUMP(SQ1,SQ2,PLAYER);
    integer   SQ1, SQ2, PLAYER;
    begin integer   S, OPPONENT;

    S := PLAYER;
    OPPONENT := -PLAYER;

    if BOARD[SQ1] = PLAYER   ∧   BOARD[SQ2] = VACANT  ∧
            ( (SQ2 = SQ1+S*8   ∧   BOARD[SQ1+S*4] = OPPONENT) ∨
              (SQ2 = SQ1+S*10  ∧   BOARD[SQ1+S*5] = OPPONENT) )
        then LEGALJUMP := true
        else LEGALJUMP := false;

    end LEGALJUMP;
```

Example 3.7 Complete, Final Kriegspiel Procedures Written in ALGOL 60

```
procedure  INITIALIZE (BOARD);   integer array BOARD;
    begin integer SQ;

    for SQ := 6 step 1 until 18 do
        begin BOARD[SQ]    := BLACK;
              BOARD[SQ+22] := RED;
        end;

    for SQ := 19 step 1 until 27 do
        BOARD[SQ] := VACANT;

    for SQ := 1 step 1 until 5 do
        BOARD[SQ] := BOARD[9*SQ-4] := BOARD[SQ+40] := ILLEGAL;

    end INITIALIZE;
```

```
procedure  OBTAIN (SQ1,SQ2);
   integer SQ1,SQ2;

   begin
     REQUEST: print ('ENTER ANOTHER MOVE');
              input (SQ1,SQ2);

              if SQ1 ≥ 1 ∧ SQ1 ≤ 32 ∧ SQ2 ≥ 1 ∧ SQ2 ≤ 32
                 then begin SQ1 := CONVERT(SQ1);
                            SQ2 := CONVERT(SQ2);

                      end
                 else begin print ('MOVE NOT ON THE BOARD');
                            goto REQUEST;
                      end;
     end OBTAIN;

integer procedure  CONVERT(SQ);
   integer SQ;

   CONVERT := if SQ ≤ 8
                 then SQ + 5
                 else if SQ ≤ 16
                      then SQ + 6
                      else if SQ ≤ 24
                           then SQ + 7
                           else SQ + 8;
     end CONVERT;

boolean procedure LEGALJUMP (SQ1,SQ2,PLAYER);
   integer SQ1,SQ2,PLAYER;

   begin integer  S, OPPONENT;

     S := PLAYER;
     OPPONENT := -PLAYER;
   if BOARD[SQ1] = PLAYER ∧ BOARD[SQ2] = VACANT ∧
        ( (SQ2 = SQ1+S*8  ∧ BOARD[SQ1+S*4] = OPPONENT) ∨
          (SQ2 = SQ1+S*10 ∧ BOARD[SQ1+S*5] = OPPONENT) )
      then LEGALJUMP := true
      else LEGALJUMP := false

   end LEGALJUMP;

procedure  UPDATEBOARD (SQ1,SQ2,PLAYER);
   integer  SQ1,SQ2,PLAYER;

   begin integer S;

     S := PLAYER;
     BOARD[SQ1] := VACANT;
     BOARD[SQ2] := PLAYER;

     if SQ2 = SQ1+S*8
        then begin print ('REMOVE PIECE ON JUMPED SQUARE');
                   BOARD[SQ1+S*4] := VACANT;
             end;
```

```
        if SQ2 = SQ1+S*10
           then begin print ('REMOVE PIECE ON JUMPED SQUARE');
                       BOARD[SQ1+S*5] := VACANT;
                end;
    end UPDATEBOARD;


boolean procedure  CANJUMP(SQ,PLAYER);
    integer SQ,PLAYER;

    begin integer S,OPPONENT;

        S := PLAYER;
        OPPONENT := -PLAYER;

        if (BOARD[SQ+S*4] = OPPONENT ∧ BOARD[SQ+S*8] = VACANT) ∨
           (BOARD[SQ+S*5] = OPPONENT ∧ BOARD[SQ+S*10] = VACANT)
           then CANJUMP := true
           else CANJUMP := false;

    end CANJUMP;


boolean procedure  NOJUMPEXISTS(PLAYER);
    integer PLAYER;

    begin integer SQ;

        NOJUMPEXISTS := true;

        for SQ := 6 step 1 until 40 do
            if BOARD[SQ] = PLAYER ∧ CANJUMP(SQ,PLAYER)
               then begin  NOJUMPEXISTS := false;
                           goto RETURN;
                    end;
        RETURN:
    end NOJUMPEXISTS;


boolean procedure  LEGALNONJUMP(SQ1,SQ2,PLAYER);
    integer SQ1,SQ2,PLAYER;

    begin integer S;

        S := PLAYER;

        if BOARD[SQ1] = PLAYER ∧ BOARD[SQ2] = VACANT ∧
           (SQ2 = SQ1+S*4 ∨ SQ2 = SQ1+S*5)
           then LEGALNONJUMP := true
           else LEGALNONJUMP := false;

    end LEGAL NONJUMP;


procedure  CONTINUETHEJUMP(SQ1,PLAYER);
    integer SQ1,PLAYER;

    begin integer SQ2;
```

```
A:    print ('FURTHER JUMP REQUIRED - ENTER NEXT SQUARE');
B:    input (SQ2);

      if SQ2 ≥ 1 ∧ SQ2 ≤ 32
         then SQ2 := CONVERT(SQ2)
         else begin print ('SQUARE OFF BOARD - TRY AGAIN');
                     goto B;
               end;

      if LEGALJUMP(SQ1,SQ2,PLAYER)
         then UPDATEBOARD (SQ1,SQ2,PLAYER)
         else begin print ('ILLEGAL SQUARE - TRY AGAIN');
                     goto B;
               end;

      if CANJUMP(SQ2,PLAYER)
         then begin SQ1 := SQ2;
                    goto A;
               end

   end CONTINUETHEJUMP;




boolean procedure ISKING ( );
   begin integer SQ;

   ISKING = false;

   for SQ := 6,7,8,9 do
        if BOARD[SQ] = RED ∨ BOARD[SQ+31] = BLACK
           then ISKING = true

   end ISKING;




boolean procedure  NOMOVE(PLAYER);
   integer PLAYER;

   begin integer S,SQ;

   NOMOVE := true;
   S := PLAYER;

   for SQ := 6 step 1 until 40 do
        if BOARD[SQ] = PLAYER ∧
           (BOARD[SQ+S*4] = VACANT ∨
              BOARD[SQ+S*5] = VACANT ∨
           CANJUMP(SQ,PLAYER))
           then begin NOMOVE := false;
                      goto RETURN;
                 end;

   RETURN:
   end NOMOVE;
```

EXERCISES

Exercise 3.1

Consider the following alternative description of P_1 for the payroll problem:

$$P_1$$

Initialize for program

10   Read the next employee card
        Process the card and check
        Update for weekly average
        <u>goto</u> 10

P_1 contains a simple (but common) error in using the top-down approach. What is the error?

Exercise 3.2   (Filling in the Top-Down Levels)

Consider the following program specification:

Input: An integer n

Output: The binomial coefficients,

$$\binom{n}{m} = n!/(n-m)! * m! = \frac{n*(n-1)8 \ldots *(n-m+1)}{m*(m-1)* \ldots *1}$$

for all values of m from 1 to n. Note: $\binom{n}{m}$ is the number of ways to select m objects out of a population of size n.

Consider also the following programs.

<u>PL/I</u>

```
P:  PROCEDURE  OPTIONS(MAIN);
    DECLARE   (I,COEF,M,N,NUM,DEN)
              FIXED;

    GET LIST(N);

    DO M = 1 TO N;

      NUM = DEN = 1;

      DO I = N BY -1 TO N-M+1;
        NUM = NUM*I;
      END;
```

<u>ALGOL 60</u>

```
begin
integer I,COEF,M,N,NUM,DEN;

read (N);

for M := 1 step 1 until N do
  begin

  NUM := DEN := 1;

  for I := N step -1 until N-M+1
    do NUM := NUM*I;
```

```
DO I = M BY -1 TO 1;
   DEN = DEN*I;
END;


COEF = NUM/DEN;
PUT LIST (N,M,COEF);

   END;

END P;
```

```
for I := M step -1 until 1
   do DEN := DEN*I;

COEF := NUM/DEN;
print (N,M,COEF);

end;


end;
```

Write the intermediate "levels" using top-down programming for expanding the problem specification into one of the given programs. (Note: Only two or three levels are needed.)

Exercise 3.3 (Using the Top-Down Approach)

Consider the following definition of the input/output characteristics of a program:

Input: A sequence of characters representing the text of a letter. The text contains only alphabetic English words, blanks, commas, periods, the special word "PP" denoting the beginning of a paragraph, and the special word "PPPP" denoting the end of the input sequence.

Output: (a) The number of words in the text
(b) The text given as input, printed according to the following format:

(1) The first line of each paragraph is to be indented five spaces and successive lines are to be left-adjusted. Lines are printed in units of 60 or fewer characters.
(2) One blank is to separate each word from the previous word, comma, or period.
(3) Any words containing more than 12 characters are to be replaced by the string "XXXXX."

Consider also the following beginning of a top-down development of the program:

$$P_0$$

process (input text);

P_1

initialize for program
REPEAT: if end of input then print number words and stop;
          process next paragraph;
          goto REPEAT;

Formalizing P_1, we obtain the following:

P_2

NOS_WORDS = 0;
TERMINATOR = empty string;
REPEAT: if TERMINATOR = 'PPPP' then print (NOS_WORDS) and stop
          process next paragraph (TERMINATOR,NOS_WORDS);
          goto REPEAT;

P_2 reflects the decision that "process next paragraph" not only processes
the next paragraph but also updates the value of the terminator to "PP" or
"PPPP" and updates the number of words. Continue the top-down
approach for the problem by:

(a) Writing the next level P_3
(b) Formalizing P_3 into P_4 so that the program of P_4 is correct and
    completely specified.

Exercise 3.4 (Pitfalls of the Bottom-Up Approach)
    To illustrate the dangers of bottom-up programming, consider the problem
    of Exercise 3.3. Suppose we decided *before* programming the problem that
    we needed a function WORD_COUNT which accepted a SENTENCE as
    an argument and returned the number of words in the sentence. Write the
    program of Exercise 3.3 using this function. Do you see the difficulty?

USE OF MNEMONIC NAMES

The importance of using good mnemonic names was briefly discussed in Proverb 10. This issue is important enough to warrant a more detailed discussion, which is given here. When writing programs it is tempting to use short, uninformative names. The temptation arises from the extra time required to devise and write illuminating (probably longer) names. Nevertheless, the choice of names has a psychological impact that cannot be ignored. Consider the two program sections in Example 4.1. Example 4.1b presents a clearer set of

Example 4.1   Use of Mnemonic Names

4.1a Poor	4.1b Better
`input (X1,X2,X3);`	`input (A,B,C);`
`X4 := sqrt (X2↑2 - 4*X1*X3);`	`DISCR    := sqrt (B↑2 - 4*A*C);`
`X5 := (-X2 + X4)/(2*X1);`	`ROOT1    := (-B + DISCR)/(2*A);`
`X6 := (-X2 - X4)/(2*X1);`	`ROOT2    := (-B - DISCR)/(2*A);`

instructions for obtaining quadratic roots, simply because of its use of the names commonly used in the familiar equation:

$$\text{Root} = (-B \pm \sqrt{B^2 - 4AC}) / 2A$$

Good mnemonic names are a powerful tool for clarity, documentation, and debugging. To reap maximum benefit from your time and effort, the psychological concepts of "set" and "distance" (Ref. W1) should be considered.

95

Psychological Set and Distance

In psychology, the term "set" means a readiness to respond to certain stimuli in a specific way. In the programming context, a "psychological set" refers to the programmer's tendency to interpret names as representing particular types of entities. Entities like social security numbers, rates of pay, people's names, and the like, have many possible representations. It is important that the psychological set activated by each name accurately reflect its value.

For example, suppose that a programmer is going to represent the following three entities: a rate of pay, a number of hours worked, and a gross pay. Assume that due to the input format the programmer chooses the identifiers COLUMN10, COLUMN20, and COLUMN30, respectively. Using these names is dangerous. Not only do they fail to reflect their true values, they can also complicate program changes. Suppose that the input format to the program was changed so that the rate of pay, hours worked, and gross pay were changed to columns 20, 30, and 10, respectively. For each name to retain its relation to the input format, the programmer must change all occurrences of COLUMN10 to COLUMN20, COLUMN20 to COLUMN30, and COLUMN30 to COLUMN10. Due to an easily made oversight, it is possible that some occurrence of the name COLUMN10, for example, might remain unchanged, since it does not semantically relate to a rate of pay. Later, the difficulty of finding such a mistake could be disastrous. Clearly the programmer should use a name like RATE_OF_PAY or PAYRATE to represent this value.

Another aspect of psychological set arises when names have no specific semantic role. For example, a programmer may define an array whose subscripts do not correspond to any meaningful object in the real world, or he may define a function of purely mathematical arguments. In these cases, a standard name should be used. For example, subscripts are generally denoted by I, J, or K, functions by F, G, or H, and arguments by X, Y, or Z. Often these familiar conventions will lend understanding. For example,

$$I = F(X,Y)$$

is more suggestive than

$$Y = X(I,F)$$

if the left-hand side denotes an integer-valued variable and the right-hand side denotes the application of a function to two arbitrary real variables.

A name that is an abbreviation for a longer conceptual unit can also be hazardous, especially when the resulting abbreviation is an acronym that activates a psychological set for another entity. For example, a programmer who desires a name for a rate of pay entry would be unwise to use the name ROPE, which does not semantically reflect the entity's true value. The temptation, of course, is to think of a long, heavy cord of intertwined fibers.

In addition to choosing a proper name for each entity, names chosen for different entities should be psychologically "distant" enough so that no confusion results. Since the distance concept is related to the psychology of the programmer, it resists formalization. Loosely speaking, names that look alike, sound alike, are spelled alike, or have similar meanings are not psychologically distant.

Consider the following pairs of names along with the indication of their distance:

	Name for one entity	Name for another entity	Distance
(a)	BKRPNT	BRKPNT	Almost invisible
(b)	MOVLT	MOVLF	Almost none
(c)	EPSILON	UPSILON	Small
(d)	EPSILON	PEPSILON	Small
(e)	OMEGA	DELTA	Large
(f)	ROOT	DISCRIMINANT	Large and informative

In this table the distance between pairs of names is small, except for entries (e) and (f). As for (a) through (d), good luck! Entry (a) shows two discrete names, but in a program could you be sure that one is not a typing or key punching error? In general, shy away from using "close" names.

Consider entry (b) which is taken from an actual program. The names had the following meanings:

Name (Argument)	Meaning
MOVLF(SQ1)	MOVE *Left From* square SQ1
MOVLT(SQ1)	MOVE *Left To* square SQ1
MOVRF(SQ1)	MOVE *Right From* square SQ1
MOVRT(SQ1)	MOVE *Right To* square SQ1

The programmer in this case wrote four functions that required a square on a checkerboard as an argument. The input square was denoted by "SQ1," and the value returned by the function was *true* or *false* depending on whether it was possible to move left or right, from or to, the square SQ1 given as input. The choice of names, good on initial consideration, resulted in a series of errors. The programmer confused MOVLF and MOVRF.

Example 4.1a also illustrates the distance concept in that the variable names X1, X2, . . ., X6 are so "close" that confusion is likely to result. Furthermore, watch out for variations in the form of a name. If you write SUBEXP in one place and SUBEX in another place, the computer will not know that they refer to the same value.

Other Factors

It is often convenient to use mnemonics to stand for constants. A familiar example is assigning 3.1415926536 to the name PI since it is simpler to write PI than to write the long string of digits. The pitfall of using names for constants is that the programmer must be absolutely certain that his constants will remain constant! If a programmer writes

F(ZERO)

where ZERO = 0.0 is an actual parameter, and in the procedure F also writes

X := X + 1

where X is the corresponding formal parameter, he has defeated the purpose of his own name.

In ALGOL 60, the free interspersing of blanks in variable names is allowed. The use of this convention should be avoided. It is difficult to maintain names like SS RATE versus SSRATE or IS KING(PLAYER) versus ISKING-(PLAYER). Furthermore, the reader of a program with such names often finds it hard to ascertain whether an expression like

(PI*OUT DIM*21.0) / NUM RPM

is legal since the blank spaces are squeezed out by a typical ALGOL 60 compiler. We may summarize the point of this section as follows:

(1)   Use names that accurately reflect their semantic roles.
(2)   Use psychologically distant names for different entities.
(3)   Use standard notational conventions where applicable.

PRETTYPRINTING

Like the use of menmonic names, the notion of "prettyprinting" (Proverb 19) is important enough to warrant a special section in this chapter. Prettyprinting should become a habit for every programmer. It is extremely simple, yet highly effective when used conscientiously. Briefly stated, prettyprinting is the spacing of a program to illuminate its logical structure. Generally, this means the *alignment* of statements that are logically grouped together and the *indentation* of local statements that are part of larger logical units.

Consider Example 4.2. Here we have two different ways to space the same procedure declaration. Example 4.2a shows the procedure written without concern for displaying its logical structure. Example 4.2b shows the same procedure prettyprinted. In the latter it is obvious that the second IF statement is part of the first, a fact that can easily be missed in a hasty reading of the first example.

Example 4.2 Prettyprinting in PL/I and ALGOL 60

4.2a. Poor	4.2b. Better

4.2a. Poor

PL/I

```
F:   PROCEDURE (X,Y);
IF   X=0   THEN
IF   Y=0   THEN   RETURN(0);
ELSE RETURN(Y+1);
ELSE RETURN(X+Y - X*Y);
END F;
```

4.2b. Better

PL/I

```
F:   PROCEDURE(X,Y);
     IF X=0
        THEN   IF Y=0
               THEN RETURN(0);
               ELSE RETURN(Y+1);
        ELSE   RETURN(X+Y - X*Y);
END F;
```

ALGOL 60

```
real procedure F(X,Y);
if X=0 then begin
if Y=0 then F := 0
else   F := Y+1 end
else   F := X+Y - X*Y
```

ALGOL 60

```
real procedure F(X,Y);
     if X=0
        then begin if Y=0
                   then F := 0
                   else F := Y+1
              end
        else F := X+Y - X*Y
```

Some prettyprinting conventions used in Example 4.2b are the following:

(1) The procedure heading and its END statement are aligned, and the body is indented to the right.
(2) The THEN and its corresponding ELSE are aligned.
(3) The THEN and ELSE of the inner statement are also further indented to show that they are sections of the outer IF statement.

Similar methods of indentation and alignment should also be used to illuminate the structure of nested loops and blocks of subordinate code. Generally speaking, comments should follow the indentation of the program but should also stand out from program statements.

Prettyprinting is a concept important enough to have influenced language design. For example, ALGOL and PL/I explicitly allow free format to stimulate the prettyprinting of programs. Although it is often not obvious, almost all higher level languages have spacing requirements flexible enough to allow prettyprinting, even if they are not specifically designed for it. It is unfortunate that programs in some languages like FORTRAN and BASIC are seldom prettyprinted.

Prettyprinting is especially important in the debugging and maintenance of programs. With good prettyprinting, it is fairly easy to detect errors like misplaced sections of code and improperly nested blocks. Furthermore, a programmer trying to read and understand the program does not have to consciously devote time to discovering the structure, an advantage that greatly reduces the difficulty in understanding the program and that makes it much easier to change should the need arise.

One difficulty in prettyprinting your program is the extra effort required. However, with judicious use of tab stops or drum cards, it takes almost no extra effort. Usually it is sufficient to indent in multiples of three to five spaces. This practice provides an easily recognized structure without requiring too much additional space.

As a further example, two complete FORTRAN programs are presented in Examples 4.3 and 4.4. The first is not prettyprinted; the second is. The programs

Example 4.3 FORTRAN Program Without Prettyprinting

```
C      THIS PROGRAM SOLVES N (N.LE.20) SIMULTANEOUS LINEAR EQUATIONS
C      IN N UNKNOWNS, USING THE GAUSS-SEIDEL ALGORITHM.
C      NOTE- NO MAIN DIAGONAL ELEMENT IS ZERO.
C      NOTE- THE ACCURACY OF A SOLUTION MATRIX X IS THE SUM OF
C      ABSOLUTE ERRORS FOR THE N EQUATIONS
       DIMENSION A(20,20),B(20),X(20)
       INTEGER ROW,COLUMN
C      READ IN NUMBER OF EQUATIONS(N), MAXIMUM ITERATIONS(MAX),
C      ACCURACY(EPSLON), COEFFICIENT MATRIX(A), AND CONSTANT MATRIX(B)
       READ(5,500) N,MAX,EPSLON
       READ(5,510 A,B
C      SET ESTIMATED SOLUTION VALUES TO ZERO
       DO 10 I=1,N
    10 X(I)=0.0
C      MAIN ALGORITHM FOLLOWS
       DO 40 ITER=1,MAX
       TOTERR=0.0
C      FOR EACH EQN,  COMPUTE TRIAL VALUE USING ESTIMATED VALUES
       DO 30 ROW=1,N
       TRIAL=0.0
       DO 20 COLUMN=1,N
    20 TRIAL=TRIAL+A(ROW,COLUMN)*X(COLUMN)
C      ADJUST ESTIMATED SOLUTION VALUES
       ERROR=B(ROW)-TRIAL
       X(ROW)=X(ROW)+ERROR/A(ROW,ROW)
    30 TOTERR=TOTERR+ABS(ERROR)
C      PRINT RESULTS IF TOTAL ERROR IS LESS THAN ACCURACY(EPSLON)
C      OTHERWISE ITERATE AGAIN
       NUMIT=ITER
       IF(TOTERR.LT.EPSLON) GO TO 50
    40 CONTINUE
C      PRINT RESULTS
    50 WRITE(6,520)
       WRITE(6,530) (I,X(I),I=1,N)
       WRITE(6,540) TOTERR,NUMIT
       STOP
   500 FORMAT(2I3,F10.7)
   510 FORMAT(8F10.5)
   520 FORMAT(1X,8X,1HI,10X,4HX(I)//)
   530 FORMAT(1X,4X,I5,5X,1PE15.8)
   540 FORMAT(1H0, 9HERROR IS ,1PE15.8,7H AFTER ,I4,12H ITERATIONS
       END
```

Example 4.4   FORTRAN Program with Prettyprinting

```
C        THIS PROGRAM SOLVES N (N.LE.20) SIMULTANEOUS LINEAR EQUATIONS IN
C        N UNKNOWNS, USING THE GAUSS-SEIDEL ALGORITHM
C        NOTE - NO MAIN DIAGONAL ELEMENT IS ZERO;  THE ACCURACY OF A SOLUTION
C              MATRIX X IS THE SUM OF ABSOLUTE ERRORS FOR THE N EQUATIONS
C
         DIMENSION  A(20,20), B(20), X(20)
         INTEGER    ROW, COLUMN
C
C        ** READ IN NUMBER OF EQUATIONS(N), MAXIMUM ITERATIONS(MAX),
C           ACCURACY(EPSLON), COEFFICIENT MATRIX(A), AND CONSTANT MATRIX(B)
C
         READ(5,500) N, MAX, EPSLON
         READ(5,510) A, B
C
C        ** SET ESTIMATED SOLUTION VALUES TO ZERO
C
         DO 10  1 = 1,N
      10     X(I) = 0.0
C
C        ** MAIN ALGORITIIM FOLLOWS
(:
         DO 40   ITER = 1,MAX
               TOTERR = 0.0
C
C              ** FOR EACH EQN, COMPUTE TRIAL VALUE USING ESTIMATED VALUES
C
               DO 30   ROW = 1,N
                  TRIAL - 0.0
                  DO 20    COLUMN = 1,N
      20              TRIAL = TRIAL + A(ROW,COLUMN)*X(COLUMN)
C
C                 ** ADJUST ESTIMATED SOLUTION VALUES
C
                  ERROR  = B(ROW) - TRIAL
                  X(ROW) = X(ROW) + ERROR/A(ROW,ROW)
                  TOTERR = TOTERR + ABS(ERROR)
      30       CONTINUE
C
C              ** PRINT RESULTS IF TOTAL ERROR IS LESS THAN ACCURACY(EPSLON)
C                 OTHERWISE ITERATE AGAIN
C
               NUMIT = ITER
               IF (TOTERR .LT. EPSLON) GOTO 50
      40 CONTINUE
C
C
C        ** PRINT RESULTS
C
      50 WRITE(6,520)
         WRITE(6,530) (I, X(I),  I = 1,N)
         WRITE(6,540) TOTERR, NUMIT
         STOP
C
     500 FORMAT (2I3, F10.7)
     510 FORMAT (8F10.5)
     520 FORMAT (1X, 8X, 1HI, 10X, 4HX(I) //)
     530 FORMAT (1X, 4X, I5, 5X, 1PE15.8)
     540 FORMAT (1H0,9HERROR IS , 1PE15.8, 7H AFTER , I4, 12H ITERATIONS.)
         END
```

solve systems of linear equations using the Gauss-Seidel algorithm. A corresponding program in BASIC is shown in Example 4.5. The use of FORTRAN and BASIC in these examples is deliberate. Even in textbooks, users of these languages are seldom (if ever) exposed to the possibilities of prettyprinting, even though almost every implementation admits great latitude in the spacing of programs.

There is one final point, namely the use of blank lines. The blank line is excellent for separating modules of the program and highlighting critical sections. Examine prettyprinted Examples 4.4 and 4.5. Note how logical sections of the program become apparent solely because of the use of blank lines.

Having said all this, we admit that there are times when prettyprinting is a liability rather than an asset. In particular, when input/output is character-oriented and very slow, as with paper tape or the slower teletype models, the time required to print extra spaces may be excessive. Or when permanent storage is utilized, the extra spaces may greatly increase the storage space required. In such cases, the structure of the programs can be made apparent by judicious use of a pencil and straight edge. If you either outline or bracket logical sections of code, it becomes fairly simple to pick out the structure.

Other equally valid methods for illuminating the logical structure of programs exist. The most important thing is not *which* method you use, but rather that you use *some* method.

REPRESENTATION OF ALGORITHMS AND TRICKY PROGRAMMING

Programmers often work with entities like dollars, dates, addresses, measurements, peoples' names, and the like. These entities have properties that differ significantly from entities like numbers and strings. Yet numbers and strings are the primitive entities of today's programming languages. Consider the difference between a "number," say 1,776, and a "date," say 1776 A.D. You can perform all the usual operations on numbers, but while you can subtract two dates to get an age, it doesn't make sense to add two dates or to take the square root of a date.

Part of the programmer's job is to map the entities he intends to work with into the representations of a particular programming language. For a language like PL/I, the range of this mapping would include numbers, strings, labels, pointers, ,offsets, and structures. Thus a programmer may choose a particular representation for an entity but may not be able to describe the entity itself or its specific properties. More importantly, the representation does not guarantee that an operation which is applicable in a programming language will have any meaning when applied to the original entity.

Example 4.5 Prettyprinting in BASIC

```
10   REM    THIS PROGRAM SOLVES N (N<21) SIMULTANEOUS
20   REM    EQUATIONS USING THE GAUSS-SEIDEL ALGORITHM
30   REM    NOTE:  NO MAIN DIAGONAL TERM IS ZERO
40   REM
50          DIM A(20,20), B(20), C(20), D(20), X(20)
100  REM
110  REM
120  REM   *INPUT NUMBER OF EQUATIONS, MAXIMUM ITERATIONS,
130  REM    ACCURACY, COEFFICIENT MATRIX, AND CONSTANT TERMS
140  REM
150         INPUT N,M,E
160         MAT INPUT A
200         MAT INPUT B
210  REM
220  REM   *SET ESTIMATED VALUES TO ZERO
230  REM
240         MAT X = ZER
250  REM
260  REM  **MAIN ALGORITHM
270  REM
280          FOR I = 1 TO M
290  REM
300  REM  **FOR EACH EQN COMPUTE TRIAL VALUE USING ESTIMATED VALUES
310             LET T = 0
320             MAT C = A*X
330             MAT D = B - C
340  REM
350  REM    /* ADJUST ESTIMATED VALUES AND COMPUTE TOTAL ERROR */
360  REM
370             FOR J = 1 TO N
400                 X(J) = X(J) + X(J)/A(J,J)
410                 T = T + ABS(D(J))
420             NEXT J
430             LET K = I
440  REM
450  REM     * STOP IF TOTAL ERROR IS LESS THAN DESIRED
460  REM       ACCURACY OTHERWISE ITERATE AGAIN
470  REM
480             IF T < E THEN 520
500         NEXT I
510  REM
520  REM    /* PRINT RESULTS */
530  REM
540             PRINT "I", "X(I)"
550             FOR I = 1 TO N
560                 PRINT I, X(I)
570             NEXT I
580             PRINT "TOTAL ERROR IS"; T; " AFTER", K, " ITERATIONS."
590             STOP
600             END
```

Consider the following line of PL/I code, for example:

$$X = (Y < Z)*4 + (Y \geq Z)*6;$$

in which the value of the expression $(Y < Z)$ is 1 if the value of Y is less than the value of Z, and 0 otherwise; similarly for $(Y \geq Z)$. Intuitively, the comparison of Y with Z yields a truth value, *true* or *false*. In many languages and computers, the condition *true* is represented by the bit pattern for 1 and *false* is represented by the bit pattern for 0.

For the above code, if Y=1 and Z=2, then

$$(Y < Z) = true = 1$$
$$(Y \geq Z) = false = 0$$

and X is thus assigned the value 4. The answer is correct, but it is hard to understand the code because it is somewhat unnatural to evaluate

$$(true * 4) + (false * 6)$$

Consider also the equivalent line of code,

IF $Y < Z$ THEN X = 4;
ELSE X = 6;

This line of code is more natural than the equivalent line above, that is, it does not depend upon the "trick" of equating *true* with 1 and *false* with 0.

The entities *true* and *false* are not the only ones that may be unnaturally used. Since numbers and letters are internally represented as bit strings, it is conceivable to add a number to a letter and come out with a number, letter, or bit string as a result. In some languages (not PL/I) the test to see if 15 + 'A' = 'P' succeeds. However, such a test is difficult to comprehend since it has no common analogue in our thinking.

More generally (see Fig. 4.1), the input to any program represents some class of real world entities: chess squares, wages, row numbers, cards, colors, and the like. A computation is required to transform these entities into other entities, for example, a chess move, an amount of money, a new row number, a card played, another color, and the like. The computer, however, can operate only in limited ways and on a limited set of entities like strings or integers. Thus, it is necessary to transform the real world set of entities and operations into a program containing computer entities and operations. We shall say that a program is "straightforward" or "natural" or "not tricky" if each step in the computer algorithm has a simple correspondence to a step in a real-world algorithm that a person would use to solve the problem. In other words, if the computer algorithm is analogous to the real-world algorithm, the program is "straightforward" or "natural."

Straightforwardness and naturalness are closely connected to the clarity and readability of programs. The programmer soon learns that one of the hardest chores of programming is understanding another programmer's code. Often programs do not accurately reflect the real world algorithm corresponding to the numerical, array, logical, or string operations that are required for their computer implementation.

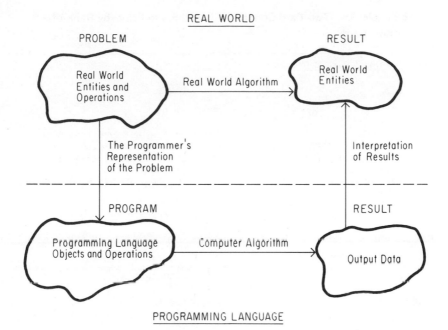

Fig. 4.1   Model for programming task

Try looking at any program that you wrote a month ago without peeking at the comments or the documentation. See if you immediately understand all of its details. Now imagine what it would be like for someone else who hadn't seen the program before. Clarity is a godsend to anyone who has to document, debug, extend, use, grade, or otherwise handle a computer program. Unless a program printout is being used by only one person, clarity is a double godsend to anyone having to use the program other than the original programmer.

For example, consider the following problem. Given a deck of 51 cards, we are asked to find the rank of the missing card (by computer, of course!). The deck is stored in a 51-element array called DECK. To make things simple, the functions CONVERT and RECONVERT are assumed to be defined. CONVERT takes the desired rank of a card as its argument and maps the rank of the card into a number: 1 (for ace), 2 (for deuce), . . ., 13 (for king). RECONVERT does the reverse operation. Example 4.6 depicts two pieces of code, both of which claim to do the job correctly. Your problem is to discover *why* each one gives the correct result.

Example 4.6b is obviously correct. In the real world, it corresponds to keeping a checklist of each rank and checking off the card ranks, one by one, until the deck is exhausted. Then the checklist is scanned to find out which card has been checked fewer than four times, and the selected rank is printed.

Example 4.6a is also correct but far less straightforward. It has almost no

Example 4.6   Two Card-Counting Algorithms to Print the Rank of a Missing Card

---

4.6a.   "Tricky" Card Count

      PL/I   ALGOL 60

```
COUNT = 0;                          COUNT := 0;

DO I = 1 TO 51;                     for I := 1 step 1 until 51 do
   RANK  = CONVERT(DECK(I));        begin RANK   := CONVERT(DECK[I]);
   COUNT = COUNT + RANK;                  COUNT := COUNT + RANK;
   IF COUNT >= 13                         if COUNT ≥ 13
      THEN COUNT = COUNT - 13;                then  COUNT := COUNT - 13;
END;                                end;

PUT LIST (RECONVERT(13-COUNT));     print (RECONVERT(13-COUNT));
```

4.6b.   "Natural" Card Count

      PL/I   ALGOL 60

```
DECLARE COUNT(13) FIXED;            integer array COUNT[1:13];
DO RANK = 1 TO 13;                  for RANK := step 1 until 13 do
   COUNT(RANK) = 0;                     COUNT[RANK] := 0;
END;
                                    for I := 1 step 1 until 51 do
DO I = 1 TO 51;                     begin RANK        := CONVERT(DECK[I]);
   RANK        = CONVERT(DECK(I));         COUNT[RANK] := COUNT[RANK]+1;
   COUNT(RANK) = COUNT(RANK) + 1;   end;
END;
                                    for RANK := 1 step 1 until 13 do
DO RANK = 1 TO 13;                     if COUNT[RANK] < 4
   IF COUNT(RANK) < 4                  then print (RECONVERT(RANK));
   THEN PUT LIST (RECONVERT(RANK));
END;
```

---

correspondence to typical card-table operations. It runs through the deck keeping a modulo 13 count of all the ranks and afterwards subtracting this count from 13 to get the rank of the missing card. If you are not convinced, try it.

As another example, suppose we have a game with N players numbered, successively, 1, 2, . . ., N. After each iteration of the game we wish to change the lead player, integer P, to the next one. The player after the Nth player is player number 1. The instructions may be coded in either of the following ways:

$$P := 1 + P*\underline{sign}\ (N-P) \qquad \underline{if}\ P < N\ \underline{then}\ \ P := P + 1$$
$$\underline{else}\ P := 1$$

The sign function evaluates to + 1 if its argument is positive, 0 if its argument is 0, and −1 if its argument is negative. The code at the left is unclear because it has no analog in the real world; one simply cannot multiply a "player" by the sign of N minus the player. In the code at the right, adding 1 to

P corresponds to shifting to the next player; when the player is the last (number N), then the cycle is repeated by setting P equal to 1.

Another area where natural programs have an advantage is that of *extendability*. Because a natural algorithm is analogous to real-world operations, extensions using these operations can often be made easily. Since a tricky algorithm usually depends on specific properties of numbers or strings, it usually cannot be applied to cases other than the original problem. Example 4.6 illustrates this point well. Say that we now wish to extend the given programs to find the ranks of N missing cards from a deck containing fewer than 51 cards.

The algorithm of Example 4.6b can be extended quite readily, as shown in Example 4.7. In the corresponding real world, the sweep of the checklist is the same as before except that when we find that a card is missing, we print it, show that we have covered it by adding it back into the checklist, and see if any others of that rank are missing.

Example 4.6a *cannot* be extended, even to cover the case of two missing cards. The validity of the algorithm is based on the condition that there is only one missing card. With only one missing card, the difference between 13 and the count must be the rank of the missing card. With two or more missing cards, the sum of the ranks of the missing cards may be split in an arbitrary number of ways. In short, this algorithm fails because it is based on the particular properties of numbers instead of the properties of cards.

One last important point about tricky or clever programming must be mentioned. There are cases where tricky methods are in fact justified; for

Example 4.7   Extension of the Card Count Problem

PL/I	ALGOL 60
| ```
DECLARE COUNT(13) FIXED;

GET LIST(N);

DO RANK = 1 TO 13;
   COUNT(RANK) = 0;
END;


DO I = 1 TO N;
   RANK = CONVERT(DECK(I));
   COUNT(RANK) = COUNT(RANK) + 1;
END;

DO RANK = 1 TO 13;
A:  IF COUNT(RANK) < 4 THEN
    BEGIN;
       PUT LIST(RECONVERT(RANK));
       COUNT(RANK) = COUNT(RANK) + 1;
       GOTO A;
    END;
END;
``` | ```
integer array COUNT[1:13];

input (N);

for RANK := 1 step 1 until 13 do
    COUNT[RANK] := 0;

for I := 1 step 1 until N do
begin RANK := CONVERT(DECK[I]);
      COUNT[RANK] := COUNT[RANK] + 1;
end;

for RANK := 1 step 1 until 13 do
A:  if COUNT[RANK] < 4 then
    begin
       print (RECONVERT(RANK));
       COUNT[RANK] := COUNT[RANK] + 1;
       goto A;
    end;
``` |

example, to get efficiency of execution or economy of storage. However, before you resort to tricky programming, you should have a clear reason for doing so. Otherwise, you should stick to operations and objects that have a natural analog in the real world.

PROCEDURES, FUNCTIONS, AND SUBROUTINES

One of the most powerful facilities in programming languages is that of the "procedure." Whereas in some languages, for example, BASIC and COBOL, the facilities for procedures are limited, all programmers can make good use of procedures. Their proper use is well-suited to developing modular, transparent programs where sections of code can be isolated and debugged separately.

In this section we shall be careful to make the following (commonly held) distinction. A "function" will refer to a procedure that returns a value. A "subroutine" will refer to a procedure that produces a change in a variable outside the procedure declaration. In particular, consider the following simple declarations:

PL/I *ALGOL 60*

```
F:   PROCEDURE(X) RETURNS(FIXED);        integer procedure F(X);
     RETURN(X*X);                            F := X*X
END  F;                                   end F
```

Here the procedure F is used as a function. For example, if the value of A is 3, an evaluation of the expression 1+F(A) yields the number 10. Consider also the following declarations:

PL/I *ALGOL 60*

```
S:   PROCEDURE(X);               procedure S(X);
     X = X*X;                        X := X*X;
END  S;                          end S
```

Here the procedure S is used as a subroutine. For example, if the value of A is 3, the statement,

PL/I   *ALGOL 60*

```
CALL S(A);        S(A);
```

results in assigning to A the value of 9.

The difference between functions and subroutines is important, but not always obvious. Generally speaking, functions are used in place of *expressions,* whereas subroutines are used in place of *statements.*

It is possible in some languages (ALGOL 60 and PL/I) to write procedures that both return a value and cause an effect outside the procedure. It is usually unwise to do this, as we will see in subsequent examples.

Functions

Loosely speaking, the *context* of a function is its relation to other sections of a program. If a function alters a quantity global to itself, then it exhibits a *context effect.* Basically, a function can produce a context effect in two ways: by altering its arguments or by altering a global variable.

Programmers who write functions with context effects can get unpleasant surprises. Consider Example 4.8. These two programs are identical except for the replacement of the expression,

$$F(B) + F(B)$$

in Example 4.8a by the expression,

$$2*F(B)$$

in Example 4.8b. These two programs are not equivalent because

$$F(B) + F(B) = (11)*(3) + (12)*(3) = 69$$
$$2 * F(B) = (2)*(11)*(3) = 66$$

Example 4.8   Context-Effect Accompanying the Returned Value of a Function

---

4.8a. One Program

PL/I

```
F:  PROCEDURE(X) RETURNS(FIXED);
    A = A + 1;
    RETURN(A*X);
END F;

A = 10;
B = 3;
C = F(B) + F(B);
PUT LIST(C);
```

ALGOL 60

```
integer procedure F(X);
    A := A + 1;
    F := A*X;
end F;

A := 10;
B := 3;
C := F(B) + F(B);
print (C);
```

4.8b. Equivalent Program?

PL/I

```
F:  PROCEDURE(X) RETURNS(FIXED);
    A = A + 1;
    RETURN(A*X);
END F;

A = 10;
B = 3;
C = 2*F(B);
PUT LIST(C);
```

ALGOL 60

```
integer procedure F(X);
    A := A + 1;
    F := A*X;
end F;

A := 10;
B := 3;
C := 2*F(B);
print (C);
```

Hence we loose a fundamental property of addition. This problem is caused by the context effect in the function F with the assignment of A+1 to A, where A is global to the function.

A similar case arises in Example 4.9. Again these examples are identical except that

$$F(B) + G(B)$$

in 4.9a is replaced by

$$G(B) + F(B)$$

in Example 4.9b. Using a left-to-right evaluation, the printed values for C, 72

Example 4.9   Violation of Commutative Property

4.9a. One Program

PL/I

```
DECLARE (A,B,C) FIXED;

F:  PROCEDURE(X) RETURNS(FIXED);
    A = A + 1;
    RETURN(A*X);
END F;

G:  PROCEDURE(X) RETURNS(FIXED);
    A = A + 2;
    RETURN(A*X);
END G;

A = 10;
B = 3;
C = F(B) + G(B);
PUT LIST(C);
```

ALGOL 60

```
integer A,B,C;

integer procedure F(X);
begin A := A + 1;
      F := A*X;
end;

integer procedure G(X);
begin A := A + 2;
      G := A*X;
end;

A := 10;
B := 3;
C := F(B) + G(B);
print (C);
```

4.9b. Equivalent Program?

PL/I

```
DECLARE (A,B,C) FIXED;

F:  PROCEDURE(X) RETURNS(FIXED);
    A = A + 1;
    RETURN(A*X);
END F;

G:  PROCEDURE(X) RETURNS(FIXED);
    A = A + 2;
    RETURN(A*X);
END G;

A = 10;
B = 3;
C = G(B) + F(B);
PUT LIST(C);
```

ALGOL 60

```
integer A,B,C;

integer procedure F(X);
begin A := A + 1;
      F := A*X;
end;

integer procedure G(X);
begin A := A + 2;
      G := A*X;
end;

A := 10;
B := 3;
C := G(B) + F(B);
print (C);
```

---

and 75, are not the same. Here, the familiar commutative property of addition is lost because of the assignment to a global variable. Certainly many programmers will be surprised to learn that F(B) + G(B) is not equivalent in this case to G(B) + F(B). Since conventional programming languages employ conventional mathematical notation, it is dangerous to write functions that violate the properties of established mathematical systems.

A further problem arises in languages where a direct "call by name" replacement of formal parameters with arguments is used. If an argument is altered by the function, a constant or an expression cannot be used as an argument, even though the value of the constant or expression may be identical to the value of the variable.

The case against context effects becomes even more severe when we need to change a program. Change is a daily occurrence in programming. Someone may find a more efficient algorithm, more output may be needed, a bug may be detected, or revised specifications may be given. If a piece of code to be changed has context effects, then these effects must be accounted for. The resulting changes may imply the need to delve deeply into the entire program for a clear understanding of what effects a function or subroutine has on other parts of the program. Adding a few extra lines of code for that desirable change may kill the correctness of another piece of code. As a result, another change may be needed to right matters, and so on. Even if this process succeeds, it is not likely to add to the clarity or flexibility of the program. Had the original program been written without context effects, the function could be changed.

Subroutines

The purpose of a subroutine is to produce some effect external to itself, not to return a value. Essentially, a subroutine consists of a group of statements isolated from a main routine or program for convenience or clarity. The problems encountered with context effects in subroutines are quite similar to those encountered in functions. There is one important exception. Since a subroutine is designed to update a specific set of variables, each of the changed variables should be included in the list of arguments. Consider Example 4.10. By using all assigned variables in the argument list in each subroutine call, the reader can speed up tracking down the changed variables since he will not have to look through the body of the subroutine.

A Larger Example

To illustrate the often subtle dangers of context effects in a more likely setting, consider the program outlined in Example 4.11. This program allows a human being to play the game of checkers against the computer. The squares on the board are assumed to be numbered 1 to 32 in the conventional way. For

Example 4.10   Context Effect in Subroutines by Assignment to a Global Variable

4.10a Poor	4.10b Better
PL/I	PL/I

```
S:  PROCEDURE(X);            S:  PROCEDURE(X,Y);
      X = 2*(X + 1);               X = 2*(X + 1);
      B = 5*X;                     Y = 5*X;
END S;                       END S;

A = 17;                      A = 17;
B = 1;                       B = 1;
CALL S(A);                   CALL S(A,B);
PUT LIST(A,B);               PUT LIST(A,B);
```

ALGOL 60	ALGOL 60

```
procedure S(X);              procedure S(X,Y);
begin                        begin
    X := 2*(X + 1);              X := 2*(X + 1);
    B := 5*X;                    Y := 5*X;
end;                         end;

A := 17;                     A := 17;
B := 1;                      B := 1;
S(A);                        S(A,B);
print (A,B);                 print (A,B);
```

Example 4.11   Outline of a Checkers Playing Program

MAIN PROGRAM

PL/I

```
P:  PROCEDURE   OPTIONS(MAIN);
DCL (MOVE(5), BOARD(1:32), N,
     RED, BLACK, YOUR_COLOR,
     PLAYER, COMPUTER)  FIXED;

/* PLACE PROCEDURES HERE */

BLACK = +1;
RED   = -1;

GET LIST(YOUR_COLOR);

IF YOUR_COLOR = BLACK
    THEN COMPUTER = RED;
    ELSE COMPUTER = BLACK;

PLAYER = BLACK;
CALL INITIALIZE(BOARD);
```

```
DO N = 1 BY 1 WHILE(MOREMOVES(PLAYER));
   IF PLAYER = COMPUTER
      THEN CALL COMPUTER_MOVE(MOVE,PLAYER);
      ELSE CALL YOUR_MOVE(MOVE,PLAYER);

   CALL UPDATE_BOARD(MOVE,PLAYER);
   PUT EDIT('MOVE NUMBER', N, 'IS',MOVE);
   PLAYER = -PLAYER;
END;

PUT LIST('WINNER IS', -PLAYER);

END;
```

ALGOL 60

```
begin
   integer array MOVE[1:5], BOARD[1:32];
   integer N,RED,BLACK,YOURCOLOR,
          PLAYER,COMPUTER;

   comment Place Procedures Here;

   BLACK := +1;
   RED   := -1;

   input (YOURCOLOR);

   if YOURCOLOR = BLACK;
      then COMPUTER := RED
      else COMPUTER := BLACK;

   PLAYER := BLACK
   INITIALIZE(BOARD);

   N := 0
   for N := N+1 while MOREMOVES(PLAYER)
   do begin
      if PLAYER = COMPUTER
         then COMPUTERMOVE(MOVE,PLAYER)
         else YOURMOVE(MOVE,PLAYER);

      UPDATEBOARD (MOVE,PLAYER);
      print ('MOVE NUMBER', N, 'IS', MOVE);
      PLAYER := -PLAYER;
   end;

   print ('THE WINNER IS', -PLAYER);

end
```

OUTLINE OF PROCEDURES

```
procedure  INITIALIZE(BOARD);
   :
   :
   set up the standard board opening
```

Example 4.11 Outline of a Checkers Playing Program (cont'd)

```
        .
        .
        .
    end;

    procedure  UPDATE_BOARD(MOVE,PLAYER);
        .
        .
        alter the board to reflect the
        MOVE made by PLAYER
        .
        .
    end;

    procedure  MOREMOVES(PLAYER);
        .
        .
        if PLAYER has more moves on the board
           then return true  ('1'B in PL/I)
           else return false ('0'B in PL/I)
        .
        .
    end;

    procedure  COMPUTER_MOVE(MOVE,PLAYER);
        .
        .
        assign to the array MOVE the best
        selected move for PLAYER
        .
        .
        .
    end;

    procedure  YOUR_MOVE(MOVE);
        .
        .
        read a move from the human opponent
        and assign it to the array MOVE
        .
        .
    end;
```

---

brevity, much of the code has been omitted. (Note: The array MOVE is assumed to contain the square numbers comprising a legal move.)

Suppose that we are asked to specify the definition of the procedure **MOREMOVES**, which takes a PLAYER (black or red) as an argument and returns the value *true* ('1'B in PL/I) if the player has more remaining moves and *false* ('0'B in PL/I) otherwise. A likely candidate for this definition is given in PL/I and ALGOL 60 as follows:

PL/I	ALGOL 60

```
MOREMOVES: PROCEDURE(PLAYER)        boolean procedure  MOREMOVES(PLAYER);
   RETURNS(BIT(1));                 integer PLAYER;
DCL PLAYER FIXED;                   begin
                                        MOREMOVES := false;
```

```
DO N = 1 BY 1 TO 32;              for N := 1 step 1 until 32 do
IF BOARD(N) = PLAYER &               if BOARD[N] = PLAYER ∧
    CANMOVE(N,PLAYER)                    CANMOVE(N,PLAYER)
    THEN RETURN ('1'B);              then begin MOREMOVES := true;
END;                                            goto RETURN;
                                             end;
RETURN('0'B);                     RETURN:

END MOREMOVES;                    end MOREMOVES;
```

The expected output for the checkers program is of the following form:

> MOVE NUMBER 1 IS (move)
> MOVE NUMBER 2 IS (move)
> MOVE NUMBER 3 IS (move)
> .
> .
> .

However, if this program is run using the definition of MOREMOVES given above, the output would be something like the following:

> MOVE NUMBER 9 IS (move)
> MOVE NUMBER 21 IS (move)
> MOVE NUMBER 5 IS (move)
> .
> .
> .

The move numbers appear almost random. *Do you see the source of the error without reading further?*

When tested in isolation, the definition of MOREMOVES appears correct. But when included in the program of Example 4.11, the output will be in error. In this case, the global variable N is used not only as the move number in the main routine but also as the looping variable in the definition of MOREMOVES. Thus, a call to MOREMOVES changes the move number N in the main routine to the first square from which the moving player has a possible move. For the first turn (black), this is always square 9; for the second turn (red), this is always square 21. After the first two turns, the value of N depends on the two moves actually made. This error would probably be extremely difficult to detect if the whole program were written out. There might be hundreds of lines of program to search through, and no reason to suspect the procedure MORE-MOVES. Errors similar to the above are common in programming and frequently take hours or even days to correct. Yet this class of errors can be totally eliminated by writing procedures without context effects. In the case of MORE-MOVES, the programmer could easily have avoided this error simply by declaring N to be a local variable as part of a standard practice of keeping context effects out of functions.

Exceptions to the Rules and Summary

There are, of course, cases where global variables and context effects may indeed be useful. For one, there may be variables and arrays whose (often used) values remain constant within the program. Making these quantities global to the entire program certainly causes no problems. The global use of the variables BLACK, RED, VACANT, and ILLEGAL in the Kriegspiel program illustrates this point.

More importantly, there may be variables and arrays whose values do change but are used in so many procedures that passing them as arguments in every call would result in a lengthy or inefficient code. The global use of the BOARD array in the Kriegspiel program illustrates this point. In such cases, it may be justifiable to make the quantities global to all procedures.

Nevertheless, global variables and context effects can cause serious problems. If they are used, they should be used sparingly. In summary, we give the following rules of thumb:

    (1)   *Functions*
        Use a function only for its returned value.
        Do not use a function when you need a subroutine.
        Do not alter formal parameters.
        Do not alter global variables.

    (2)   *Subroutines*
        Do not use a subroutine when you need a function.
        Do not alter global variables.

    (3)   *Both*
        Do not be afraid to use local variables.

RECURSION

Loosely speaking, recursion is a method of definition in which the object being defined is used within the definition. For example, consider the following definition of the word "descendant":

A descendant of a person is a son or daughter of the person, or a descendant of a son or daughter.

In this definition *all* the descendants of the person are simply and precisely accounted for. A nonrecursive definition of "descendant" that takes all possibilities into consideration would be the following:

A descendant of a person is a son or daughter of the person, or a grandson or granddaughter of the person, or a great-grandson or great-granddaughter of the person, etc.

In this case, the definition is lengthier and less succinct than the recursive definition. It is interesting to note how dictionaries attempt to skirt recursion in the definition of "descendant." "Descendant" is often defined in terms of "ancestor," whereas "ancestor" is defined in terms of "descendant." The two definitions are, in fact, effectively recursive.

In programming, recursive definitions apply to procedure declarations. A recursive procedure declaration is one that has the potential to invoke itself. In other words, it is defined partially in terms of itself.

It seems unfortunate that recursion is so little understood in most programming circles. There is, of course, the occasional programmer who tries to write every program recursively, but by and large most programmers ignore recursion altogether.

The use of the word "unfortunate" above needs explanation. Recursive definitions are more prevalent than it might seem. The definition of ALGOL 60 states that a block is a sequence of declarations and statements, but a statement can be a block. In PL/I, arithmetic expressions are defined in terms of arithmetic primaries, which in turn are partially defined in terms of arithmetic expressions. In mathematics, recursive definitions abound.

If recursion is used regularly in areas related to programming, why is it so little used in programs themselves? First, not every language is equipped to handle recursion, and in many languages where recursion is included, it is often inefficient. Second, it is possible to write any program nonrecursively, that is, using iterative rather than recursive schemes.

The primary point of this section is that in many instances recursive definitions are clearer, more succinct, or more natural, than their nonrecursive counterparts, even if they are less efficient.

Suppose we wish to sum the elements of an array. Simple arithmetic gives us the following equality:

$$\sum_{i=1}^{n} a_i = a_1 \qquad\qquad \text{if } n = 1$$

$$\sum_{i=1}^{n} a_i = a_n + \sum_{i=1}^{n-1} a_i \qquad \text{if } n \geqslant 2$$

Stated in English, the sum of the elements of an array is the last element plus the sum of the first $n - 1$ elements. If the array has only one element, the sum is the single element. With these facts in mind, it is possible to write the function SUM recursively, as in Example 4.12a. Its nonrecursive counterpart is given in Example 4.12b.

To insure that the recursive definition of SUM is understood, observe the following analysis of the procedure when applied to a four-element array containing the numbers 3, 8, 6, and 2.

Example 4.12   Recursive and Nonrecursive Definitions of SUM

4.12a   Recursive Definition

PL/I

```
SUM:   PROCEDURE(A,N)   RECURSIVE
       RETURNS(FIXED);
       DECLARE (N,A(N)) FIXED;

       IF N = 1
           THEN RETURN(A(1));
           ELSE RETURN(A(N) + SUM(A,N-1));
END;
```

ALGOL 60

```
integer procedure SUM(A,N);
   integer N; integer array A;

   if N = 1
      then SUM := A[1]
      else SUM := A[N] + SUM(A,N-1);
```

4.12b   Nonrecursive Definition

PL/I

```
SUM:   PROCEDURE(A,N)
       RETURNS(FIXED);
       DCL (N,A(N),X) FIXED;

       X = 0;
       DO I = 1 BY 1 TO N;
          X = X + A(I);
       END;
       RETURN(X);
END;
```

ALGOL 60

```
integer procedure   SUM(A,N);
   integer N;  integer array A;
   begin integer X;
   X := 0;
   for I := 1 step 1 until N
   do  X := X + A[I];
   SUM := X;
   end;
```

Depth of Recursive Calls	*Value of SUM*
1	SUM(A,4)
2	2 + SUM(A,3)
3	2 + (8 + SUM(A,2))
4	2 + (8 + (6 + SUM(A,1)))
4	2 + (8 + (6 + 3))
3	2 + (8 + 9)
2	2 + 17
1	19

As shown, SUM is invoked four times and the final returned value is 19.

An example particularly well suited to recursive definition is the implementation of Euclid's algorithm for computing the greatest common divisor of two positive integers, X and Y. The GCD procedure requires an additional procedure REM that returns the remainder when X is divided by Y.

The definitions are shown in Example 4.13. For comparison, nonrecursive definitions of the procedures are also given.

Example 4.13   Euclid's Algorithm Programmed With and Without Recursion

---

4.13a Recursive Definition	4.13b Nonrecursive Definition

PL/I

```
GCD:  PROCEDURE (X,Y) RECURSIVE
          RETURNS(FIXED);
      DCL (X,Y,R) FIXED;

      IF X < Y
          THEN RETURN (GCD(Y,X));
      R = REM(X,Y);
      IF R = 0
          THEN RETURN (Y);
          ELSE RETURN(GCD(Y,R));

END GCD;
```

PL/I

```
GCD:  PROCEDURE(X,Y)
          RETURNS(FIXED);
      DCL (X,Y,R,T) FIXED;

      IF X < Y THEN
          BEGIN;
             T = X;
             X = Y;
             Y = T;
          END;
      R = Y;

      DO WHILE (R > 0);
          R = REM(X,Y);
          X = Y;
          Y = R;
      END;
      RETURN(X);

END GCD;
```

ALGOL 60

```
integer procedure GCD(X,Y);
integer X,Y;
begin integer R;

   if X < Y
       then GCD := GCD(Y,X);
   R := REM(X,Y);
   if R = 0
       then GCD := Y
       else GCD := GCD(Y,R);

end GCD;
```

ALGOL 60

```
integer procedure GCD(X,Y);
integer X,Y;
begin integer R,T;

   if X < Y then
       begin T := X;
             X := Y;
             Y := T;
       end;

   for R := REM(X,Y)
       while (R > 0) do
       begin X := Y;
             Y := R;
       end;
   GCD := Y;

end GCD;
```

Merely knowing what recursion looks like is not enough. It is also necessary to know (1) if recursion is applicable to the problem at hand, and (2) how to apply it. There are no formal rules in either case, but there are some guidelines. One is that the notion of mathematical "induction" is a close analog to recursion. Induction is a method of definition in which (1) initial values of a function are defined explicitly (the base step), and (2) other values are implicitly defined in terms of previous values (the inductive step). If the definition given in the second step applies to all elements other than the initial values, then the principle of mathematical induction asserts that the function is (explicitly) well-defined for all values in its domain.

To illustrate the method of inductive definition, consider the sequence of Fibonacci numbers. The first two numbers are 0 and 1, and each successive number in the sequence is the sum of the two preceding numbers. More explicitly,

$$N = 1 \quad \text{BASE STEP} \qquad F(1) = 0$$
$$N = 2 \qquad\qquad\qquad\qquad F(2) = 1$$

$$N \geqslant 3 \quad \text{INDUCTIVE STEP} \qquad F(N) = F(N-1) + F(N-2)$$

The step from this inductive definition to a recursive procedure declaration is small. A procedure to generate the Nth Fibonacci number is shown defined recursively and nonrecursively in Example 4.14. The Fibonacci procedure written recursively parrots the inductive definition and clearly shows the main property of the Fibonacci numbers. While the nonrecursive example uses the same property, it is harder to detect. The additional code required to write the function nonrecursively is mostly bookkeeping. Also note that in the recursive definition, the procedure FIB is recursively invoked twice. Without a good optimizing compiler, this double invocation is quite inefficient.

Example 4.14 Definitions of a Fibonacci Number Generator

4.14a. Recursive Definition   4.14b. Nonrecursive Definition

     PL/I   PL/I

```
FIB:  PROCEDURE(N)  RECURSIVE        FIB:  PROCEDURE(N)
      RETURNS(FIXED);                      RETURNS(FIXED);
      DCL N FIXED;                         DCL (N,I,T,F1,F2) FIXED;

      IF N <= 2                            IF N <= 2 THEN RETURN(1);
         THEN RETURN(1);                   F1 = 0;
         ELSE RETURN(FIB(N-1)+FIB(N-2));   F2 = 1;
END FIB;                                   DO I = 3 BY 1 TO N;
                                              T = F1 + F2;
                                              F1 = F2;
                                              F2 = T;
                                           END;
                                           RETURN(T);

                                     END FIB;
```

ALGOL 60	ALGOL 60

```
integer procedure FIB(N);
integer N;
    if N ≤ 2
        then FIB := 1
        else FIB := FIB(N-1) + FIB(N-2)
end FIB;
```

```
integer procedure FIB(N);
integer N;
begin integer I,T,F1,F2;

    if N ≤ 2
        then FIB := 1
    else begin
            F1 := 0;
            F2 := 1;
            for I := 3 step 1 until N
            do begin T := F1 + F2;
                     F1 := F2;
                     F2 := T;
              end;
        FIB := T;
    end

end FIB;
```

A great deal could be said about recursion, and a good deal of the literature is devoted to the subject. For our purposes, the point is simple. Explore the use of recursion. It can be a valuable part of your programming repertoire.

DEBUGGING TECHNIQUES

It may seem contradictory to include a section on debugging techniques in a work devoted to error-free programming, but we must admit that human beings are error prone. Even with maximum effort, errors may arise. Debugging is the process of finding and correcting these errors.

Top-Down Debugging

We have advocated the top-down approach to program development. In turn, we advocate the top-down approach to debugging, that is, testing the main program and the upper levels first and the most primitive modules last.

Debugging top-down should seem obvious, especially if a program has been written top-down. Programs of this type are usually well modularized, and it is unwise to debug lower levels if the upper levels may be incorrect. This means that sections of the program are integral units that can stand on their own, and the most important ones should be debugged first. A schematic illustration of a program is shown in Fig. 4.2. Encircled sections indicate that the set of enclosed modules is to be considered as a unit. The program have five main modules, each of which can be debugged separately. Some of these modules call submodules, which in turn call other more deeply nested modules. The debugging process

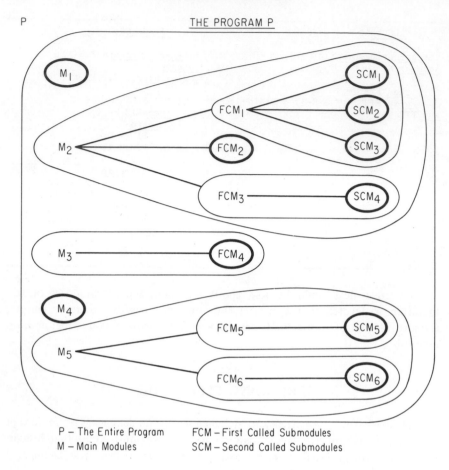

P

THE PROGRAM P

P – The Entire Program   FCM – First Called Submodules
M – Main Modules   SCM – Second Called Submodules

Fig. 4.2   Outline of a program designed top-down

starts at the topmost modules. As upper modules are verified, debugging advances to lower levels until the entire program has been debugged.

Debugging the complete program in one lump sum is to be avoided. It is akin to finding the proverbial needle in the haystack, inviting hours of extra debugging time and pages of cryptic diagnostic messages. Inevitably, this leads to the "band-aid" approach, in which pieces of code are patched and the real problems are overlooked.

Debugging facilities fall into two categories: those that are part of a language and those that are a part of your system. The programmer would be well advised to familiarize himself with both.

Language Debugging Aids

What are some of the available language debugging aids? Foremost, try to write programs that run correctly the first time. Adhere to good programming principles. The better the quality of the program to begin with, the less likely a serious error will occur, and the more likely you can find those that do.

Second, judicious use of print statements can create an external record of the operation of your program. Consider Example 4.15, a BASIC program to sum the first N integers for M different values of N. Clearly the answers

Example 4.15 Use of PRINT Statement for Debugging

Program

```
10   REM     SUM THE FIRST N INTEGERS FOR M INPUT VALUES OF N
20   LET S = 0
30   READ M
40   FOR I = 1 TO M
50       READ N
60       FOR J = 1 TO N
70           LET S = S + J
80       NEXT J
90       PRINT "SUM OF FIRST"; N; " INTEGERS IS"; S
100  NEXT I
110  STOP
120  DATA 2
130  DATA 6,3
140  END
```

Output

```
SUM OF FIRST 6 INTEGERS IS 21
SUM OF FIRST 3 INTEGERS IS 27
```

Debug line

```
 75  PRINT "ITERATION "; J; " SUM"; S
```

Output with debug line

```
ITERATION 1 SUM 1
ITERATION 2 SUM 3
ITERATION 3 SUM 6
ITERATION 4 SUM 10
ITERATION 5 SUM 15
ITERATION 6 SUM 21
SUM OF FIRST 6 INTEGERS IS 21
ITERATION 1 SUM 22
ITERATION 2 SUM 24
ITERATION 3 SUM 27
SUM OF FIRST 3 INTEGERS IS 27
```

generated by the program are incorrect. The programmer decides to check the main program loop and inserts line 75 to print out the loop variable and the current value of the sum. When the revised program is run, he sees that on iteration 1 for the second value of N the sum is already 22, that is, S is not properly initialized. Moving line 20 to line 45 solves the problem.

Essentially, the print statement is used to "dump" values of important variables so that they can be checked by hand. In this capacity, it is especially useful in procedures, and particularly recursive procedures.

Some languages supply explicit debugging facilities that enable the programmer to include statements that do not affect the logical structure of a program but that make available information about the program execution. PL/I is a clear case. The facilities for ON-conditions provide a significant debugging facility. The PL/I programmer is well-advised to explore this feature.

One of the most popular debugging aids available in several implementations is the "trace." Basically, a trace is a facility to monitor the behavior of prespecified variables or functions. The trace of a variable may monitor any use or change of its value. The trace of a function may monitor each call, its arguments, and its returned value. The programmer may use a trace to verify that his functions are being called with proper arguments and correct returned values. In function-oriented programs or programs with recursion, traces can be invaluable. One word of caution: Overuse of the trace feature has been known to produce voluminous output with no useful information.

System Debugging Aids

One simple but useful system debugging aid is the "record of control," which states where execution terminates. The value of a record of control is that it enables the programmer to pinpoint unusual error conditions or infinite loops.

Dumps are probably the oldest and best known debugging aid. Before the advent of high-level languages, machine code could be "dumped" onto paper for examination. Basically, dumps still work the same way but usually require a knowledge of the machine or assembler language. Often the programmer must also understand the associated maps and tables that tell him exactly what his dump means.

In some implementations, dumps are more in tune with a given language. The programmer may specify that the value of certain variables are to be printed on abnormal termination. The system then prints a list of the variable names and their associated values. These may be sufficient for the location of the errors.

Some systems have other aids to help the programmer, among them traps and diagnostic messages. Diagnostics are everybody's friend and enemy. This contradiction reflects the diversity of different systems.

The programmer welcomes a message like:

UNDEFINED VARIABLE X AT STATEMENT 790

but curses messages like

I EK640I COVERAGE BY BASE REGISTER 12 IN
OBJECT MODULE EXCEEDED

As debugging aids, traps usually surprise the programmer. There are a large number of trap conditions, but the best known are the overflow and underflow. An overflow occurs whenever an attempt is made to increase the value of a number beyond the size the machine can store. If 99999 is the longest decimal number that can be stored and a program exceeds this value, an overflow condition occurs. The program is "trapped," and the system prints out a message, usually terminating the program. Other traps include Input/Output traps, clock traps, and interrupts.

In summary, you can and should make good use of the debugging facilities in your language and system. They can be an invaluable tool in mastering the art of computer programming.

SOME PARTING COMMENTS

I would like to close this final chapter with a variety of thoughts on the notion of software quality. These thoughts have been partially expressed in previous chapters. They are neither new nor rigorously supported, but they do sum up a number of important issues.

Programmers are faced with numerous difficult problems. One point often confused is the difference between problem solving and programming. "Problem solving" can be viewed as the act of developing an algorithm to solve a given problem, "programming" as the act of transforming an algorithm into the linguistic concepts of a given programming language. In its conception, this book is primarily about programming, not problem solving. The techniques discussed in it will not necessarily help the programmer find a more efficient method of sorting, a fast method for computing Fourier Transforms, or a good heuristic for a chess-playing program.

The programmer's task is usually an intricate combination of both problem solving and programming. The issues in problem solving are vital to writing effective computer programs. Yet it is now well recognized that the "programming" of a given algorithm is far from trivial, and that the programmer should use all the available techniques of programming to insure that his devised algorithm is clear. While good programming techniques will offer strong guidelines for the development of a good solution to a problem, we must admit that "programming," as conceived here, is only part of the programmer's task.

A somewhat controversial issue treated in this work is that of avoiding GOTO statements. The case against the GOTO is primarily due to the concentration that it entails on the flow of control rather than on the basic computations, functions, and procedures needed to solve a given problem. Although it would probably be wise to recommend that future languages provide alternatives to the GOTO, in current languages the GOTO does exist, and in some languages it is indeed hard to avoid.

The real issue for the programmer is how to manage the complexity of his program. The indiscriminate use of the GOTO is clearly to be avoided, for its abuse can easily make a given algorithm opaque. Yet when wisely used, the GOTO can be just as transparent as alternative control structures. Our final recommendation: Use the GOTO, but use it sparingly.

As mentioned in Chapter 1, the use of flow charts has mainly been avoided in this text. As a method of program *design*, flow charts have been highly overestimated. The top-down approach to programming suppresses the use of flow charts in favor of highlighting a functional or procedural approach to program design. The case against flow charts is similar to the case against the GOTO. Flow charts can easily lead the user to a highly sequential mode of thinking. Furthermore, there is a tendency to think that once a flow chart is designed, the programming process is just about completed. Unfortunately, this is seldom the case. The programmer would be well-advised to try another approach whenever he thinks a flow chart is needed.

Consider the Kriegspiel program of Chapter 3. In this program no complete module requires a listing of more than one page of text. This characteristic results from human engineering. We all know how difficult it can be to follow a long program. In any lengthy program, we usually try to abstract a logical portion of it that will give us an indication of its overall computation. The programmer himself should recognize this fact and write his program so that each logical unit is clearly isolated on a page or less. Furthermore, as mentioned above, each unit should be definable in terms of simple input/output coordinates, avoiding the excessive use of COMMON or global variables, for these can easily destroy the real modularity of logical units.

An issue of notable prominence today is that of mathematically proving the correctness of programs. The use of correctness techniques (where a program is *certified* to contain no errors) is in sharp contrast to debugging (where a program is *observed* to contain no detectable errors). Unfortunately, the art of program correctness techniques hasn't been developed to the point where formal correctness can replace debugging as a practical programming tool. Nevertheless, an attempt to prove a program correct can provide valuable insights into the factor influencing program complexity. A programmer should write his programs so clearly that a proof of correctness as well as debugging can be performed in a straightforward manner. It does not seem unwise to recommend that every programmer should try at least once to prove formally the correctness of one of his programs. The works of Robert Floyd, Ralph London, and C.A.R. Hoare should provide a good introduction to the techniques of mathematical proofs.

One underestimated problem in programming is that of keeping to language standards. Admittedly, our languages are so diffuse in scope and often so lacking in transparent linguistic features that it is hard not to introduce or use features that make up for some of the shortcomings. For example, the lack of a simple quote convention for Hollerith strings in standard FORTRAN, the lack of a RETURN statement in ALGOL 60 procedures, and the lack of a simple exit convention from PL/I DO groups deserve remedy. Yet if we are to insist that programs are to be portable or that users can understand the programs written in other implementations, then we must stick to language features that are common to most (if not all) implementations. Even in writing a book such as this, the problem of keeping to a "standard" was difficult. Despite the difficulty, two points are worth mentioning. We should encourage the development of *more* and *better* standard defintions, and, unless there is a compelling reason to do otherwise, we should adhere to the standards we have.

One difficulty, not often felt by programmers using PL/I, ALGOL 60, or several other languages, is the often defeating cycle of arguments promulgating the use of FORTRAN. The cycle goes something like this. We want to teach prospective programmers a language that will be of practical value. While other languages may be more useful or powerful, FORTRAN is by far the most commonly used. If we don't use FORTRAN, prospective employers will not be sure of what the programmer knows. Therefore we should keep to FORTRAN.

This cycle in part sums up the circumstances for the wide use of FORTRAN. Yet, if we view the computer-based professions as about thirty years old, FORTRAN, as originally conceived, is only about fifteen years old, half the lifespan of modern computer science. FORTRAN clearly lacks a good *if-then-else* structure, a facility for grouping compound statements, alphabetic statement labels, a facility for data structures, and numerous, now well-accepted control structures. Have we learned so little in recent years that we cannot break this cycle? I hope not.

In recent years three notable efforts have occurred in the attempt to provide a significantly more effective, widely accepted computer language. The PL/I language was introduced with the hope that it would soon become familiar to most programmers and replace its predecessor, FORTRAN. Unfortunately, PL/I is so complex that it is difficult to learn and difficult to implement at a low cost. The ALGOL 68 language was introduced in the attempt to eliminate the shortcomings of ALGOL 60 and introduce important new linguistic concepts. The ALGOL 68 effort has been plagued by an overly complex definition and the lack of wider participation in its design. The recent effort (see Ref. Z6) to develop a new standard FORTRAN aims at a more powerful direct successor to FORTRAN IV. This effort is unfortunately hampered by the desire to be upwards compatible with the existing definition of FORTRAN IV. Despite these three notable attempts, it appears that it will be some years hence before a well-structured, mathematically sound, and easily learnable new language becomes commonplace.

The organization of numerous programmers into an effective programming team is a subject that deserves much investigation. Large-scale systems requiring thousands of lines of code are now commonplace. The notion that the requirements of a successful, large programming product can be met simply by rapid staffing with large numbers of programmers is now obsolete. Large amounts of debugging time and poor code have resulted from a lack of careful analysis, design, and staffing. The concept of a "chief programmer team" advocated by Mills and Baker (see Ref. B1) has had some strong initial success. Considering the importance of large systems, it is clearly worth the investment to try to develop innovative approaches to large programming projects.

There are many other related issues that could be discussed here. Among these are the need for better documentation of programs and programming languages, the development of new languages, the issue of sound control structures, and the importance of formal definitions of languages. The overriding issue is the critical need to upgrade the entire programming effort. With all of the new interest in programming, progress is certainly on its way.

EXERCISES

Exercise 4.1 (Use Mnemonic Identifiers)

In considering the creation of the proper psychological set for identifiers, the programmer must guard against using identifiers whose relationships with their values is vague, tenuous, or peculiar to the programmer himself. The purpose of the following program segment has been obscured by the use of mnemonic identifiers and intermediate variables that appear reasonable at first glance but that are in fact misleading and confusing. State the purpose of this segment. What quantity is represented by "INTER"? Rewrite the segment using a better choice of mnemonic identifiers and intermediate variables.

PL/I

```
DCL   (NUM,DENOM,RATE,INTER,
       A(1:2, 1:2))  FLOAT;

GET LIST(A);

IF A(1,1) = A(2,1) THEN
    BEGIN; PUT LIST('NO VALUE');
         STOP;
    END;

NUM   = A(1,2) - A(2,2);
DENOM = A(1,1) - A(2,1);
RATE  = NUM/DENOM;
INTER = A(1,2) - RATE*A(1,1);
PUT LIST('ANSWER IS', INTER);
```

ALGOL 60

```
real NUM,DENOM,RATE,INTER
real array A[1:2, 1:2]

input A;

if A[1,1] = A[2,1] then
    begin print ('NO VALUE');
         stop;
    end;
NUM   := A[1,2] - A[2,2];
DENOM := A[1,1] - A[2,1];
RATE  := NUM/DENOM;
INTER := A[1,2] - RATE*A[1,1];
print ('ANSWER IS', INTER);
```

Exercise 4.2 (Use of Psychologically "Distant" Identifiers)
Consider the following program specification:

> *input:* three pairs of integers denoting the co-ordinates of three points
> on a grid.
> *output:* the area of the triangle defined by the three points.

Write such a program using *only* the identifiers X1, X2, X3, . . .

Exercise 4.3 (Context Effects)
What is printed by the following piece of code?

```
            PL/I                                  ALGOL 60

BEGIN;                                begin
  DCL B FLOAT ;                          real B;

  F:  PROCEDURE(X);                      real procedure F(X);
      X = X + G(X);                      begin X := X + G(X);
      RETURN(2*X);                             F := 2*X;
  END F;                                 end;

  G:  PROCEDURE(X);                      real procedure G(X);
      X = 2*(X+1);                       begin X := 2*(X+1);
      RETURN(2*X);                             G := 2*X;
  END G;                                 end;

  B = 1;                                 B := 1;
  PUT LIST(F(F(B))+B);                   print (F(F(B))+B);

END;                                  end;
```

Exercise 4.4 (Recursion)
Rewrite CONTINUE THE JUMP of the Kriegspiel program recursively,
eliminating all GOTO's.

Exercise 4.5
There once was a frog named Mr. Croak who was beset with three
daughters of marriageable age, Ribbit1, Ribbit2, and Ribbit3. Now the
only eligible male frog, Horatio, fell for Ribbit2 and proceeded to ask for
her leg in marriage. However, Mr. Croak, concerned with the marriage
prospects for Ribbit1 and Ribbit3, proposed the following: Whichever one
of his daughters leaped the farthest would become Horatio's wife. Now,
Horatio knew, but Mr. Croak didn't, that Ribbit1 could jump three lily
pads, that Ribbit2 could jump twice as far as Ribbit1, and that Ribbit3
could jump only one third as far as Ribbit2. Thus Horatio readily agreed
and persuaded Mr. Croak that the following computer program should
determine who would wed him. (Note: R1,R2, and R3 denote the heights
of the jumps of Ribbits 1,2, and 3).

<u>PL/I</u>

```
P:  PROCEDURE  OPTIONS(MAIN);
    DCL  (R1,R2,R3) FIXED;

    F:  PROCEDURE (X)
        RETURNS(FIXED);
        X = 2*X;
        RETURN (X);
    END F;

    G:  PROCEDURE (X)
        RETURNS(FIXED);
        X = (1/3)*X;
        RETURN(X);
    END G;

R1 = 3;
R2 = F(R1);
R3 = G(R2);

PUT LIST("RIBBIT1=", R1,
         "RIBBIT2=", R2,
         "RIBBIT3=", R3);
END P;
```

<u>ALGOL 60</u>

```
begin
  integer R1,R2,R3;
  integer procedure F(X);
  integer procedure F(X);
    begin
        X := 2*X;
        F := X;

    end F;

  integer procedure  G(X);
    begin
        X := (1/3)*X;
        G := X;
    end G;

R1 := 3;
R2 := F(R1);
R3 := G(R2);

print ("RIBBIT1=", R1,
       "RIBBIT2=", R2,
       "RIBBIT3=", R3);
end;
```

What proverb is the moral of the story?

BIBLIOGRAPHY

(B1) Baker, F. T., "Chief Programmer Team Management of Production Programming," *IBM Systems Journal,* vol. 11, No. 1, 1972.

(B2) Buxton, J.N., and Randell, B., eds., "Software Engineering Techniques,"
Report on a conference sponsored by the NATO Science Committee,
Rome, Italy, October 27-31, 1969 (available from Scientific Affairs Div.,
NATO, Brussels 39, Belgium).

(C1) Cooper, Laura, and Smith, Marilyn, *Standard FORTRAN: A Problem
Solving Approach,* Houghton Mifflin, Boston, 1973.

(D1) Dahl, O.J., Dijkstra, E.W., and Hoare, C.A.R., *Structured Programming,*
Academic Press, New York, 1972.

(D2) Dijkstra, Edsgar W., "Goto Statement Considered Harmful," *Communications of the ACM,* vol. 11, No. 3, Mar. 1968.

(D3) Dijkstra, Edsgar W., "The Humble Programmer," 1972 Turing Award
Lecture, *Communications of the ACM,* vol. 15, No. 10, Oct. 1972.

(E1) Ershov, Andrei P. "Aesthetics and the Human Factor in Programming,"
Communications of the ACM, vol. 15, No. 7, July 1972, pp. 501-505.

(G1) Griswold, R., Poage, J., Polonsky, I., *The SNOBOL 4 Programming
Language,* Prentice-Hall, Englewood Cliffs, N.J., 1971.

(G2) Gross, Jonathan L., and Brainerd, Walter S., *FUNdamental PROGRAM-
MING Concepts,* Harper and Row, N.Y., 1972.

(H1) Henderson, P., and Snowdon, R. "An Experiment in Structured Programming," BIT 12, 1972.

(K1) Kemeny, John, and Kurtz, Thomas, *BASIC Programming,* 3rd ed., John
Wiley and Sons, N.Y., 1972.

(K2) Knuth, Donald E., *The Art of Computer Programming,* vol. 1, *Fundamental Algorithms,* Addison-Wesley, Reading, Mass., 1968.

(L1) Ledgard, Henry F., "Ten Mini-Languages: A Study of Topical Issues in
Programming Languages," *Computing Surveys,* vol. 3, No. 3, Sept. 1971,
pp. 115-146.

(M1) McCarthy, John, Abrahams, P., Edwards, D., Hart, T., and Levin, M.,
LISP 1.5 Programmers Manual, MIT Press, Cambridge, Mass., 1962.

(M2) McCracken, Daniel D., *A Guide to FORTRAN IV Programming,* John
Wiley and Sons, N.Y., 1972.

(M3) Mills, Harlan B., *Mathematical Foundations for Structured Programming,*
Technical Report, FSC 72-6012, IBM Federal Systems Division, Gaithersburg, Md., 1972.

(N1) Naur, Peter, ed., "Revised Report on the Algorithmic Language ALGOL
60," *Communications of the ACM,* vol. 6, No. 1, Jan. 1963.

(P1)   Parnas, David L., "A Technique for Software Module Specification With Examples," *Communications of the ACM*, vol. 15, No. 5, May 1972.

(R1)   Rustin, Randall, ed., "Debugging Techniques in Large Systems," *Proceedings of Courant Computer Science Symposium 1*, New York University, June 29-July 1, 1970, Prentice-Hall, Englewood Cliffs, N.J., 1971.

(S1)   Strachey, Christopher, "Systems Analysis and Programming," in *Computers and Computation*, Readings from *Scientific American*, W. H. Freeman & Co., San Francisco, 1971.

(S2)   Strunk, William Jr., and White, E.B., *The Elements of Style*, Macmillan, N.Y., 1970.

(W1)   Weinberg, Gerald M., *The Psychology of Computer Programming*, Van Nostrand Reinhold, N.Y., 1971.

(W2)   Weinberg, Gerald M., *PL/I Programming, A Manual of Style*, McGraw-Hill, N.Y., 1970.

(W3)   Weinberg, Gerald M., Yasukawa, N., and Marcus, R., *Structured Programming in PL/C*, Wiley, N.Y., 1973.

(W4)   Wirth, Niklaus, "Program Development by Stepwise Refinement," *Communications of the ACM*, vol. 14, No. 4, Apr. 1971, pp. 221-227.

(Z1)   _____ *Proceedings of an ACM Conference on Proving Assertions About Programs*, Las Cruces, N.M., Jan. 6-7, 1972, SIGPLAN Notices 7, No. 1, Jan. 1972, and SIGACT News, No. 14, Jan. 1972.

(Z2)   _____ *Control Structures in Programming Languages*, SIGPLAN Notices, vol. 7, No. 11, Nov. 1972.

(Z3)   _____ *PL/I(F) Language Reference Manual*, IBM System/360 Operating System, GC 28-8201-3.

(Z4)   _____ *American Standard FORTRAN*, USA Standards Institute, 1966.

(Z5)   _____ *FORTRAN IV Language*, IBM System/360 and System/370, GC28-6515-8, 1971.

(Z6)   _____ Proposed New FORTRAN Standard, American National Standards Institute committee, Interim Report, 1973.

(Z7)   _____ *COBOL Language*, IBM System/360 Operating System, C28-6516-8.

INDEX

ALGOL, 68, 127
Algorithms, 6, 10, 102
APL, 50
Arrays, 116, 117

BASIC, 20, 25, 33, 40, 49, 71, 74, 99, 102, 108, 123
Bottom-up approach, 13, 94
Bubble sort algorithm, 22f

Card problems, 36, 105
Checkers problem, 111f
COBOL, 25, 28, 71, 75, 108
Coding, 14, 15, 42
Comments, 40ff, 105
Commutative property, 110f
Constants, mnemonic names used for, 98
Constants within a loop, recomputing, 32
Context effects, 109ff, 115, 116, 129

Data connections, 16
Data representation, 15, 81
Debugging, 11, 36f, 95, 121ff
    of system, 124f
Defining problems, 5ff, 11, 64
Diagnostic messages, 124
Documentation, 40, 43f, 95, 105
Dumps, selective, 37, 124

Euclid's algorithm, 118f
"Extended" BASIC, 33, 34

Fibonacci sequence, 120
Flow charts, 2, 126

FORTRAN, 27, 28, 42, 49, 50, 71, 73, 98, 99, 100, 101, 127f
Functions, 19, 108, 109, 116

Gauss-Seidel algorithm, 102
GOTO's, use of, 19f, 22, 125f

Hand-checking, 44f

Imitation approach, 13, 14
Implementation-dependent features, 33f
Indentation, 98
Inductive definition, 119f
Initialization errors, 38f
Input/output characteristics, 6, 11, 43
Inside-out approach, 13, 14
Insurance problem, 53

Kriegspiel checkers, 77f

Language independence, 11, 64
Language standards, 126
Levels, designing in, 11, 64
Linear approach, 10, 13, 14
LISP, 37, 50
Looping constructs, 19

Mnemonic names, 27f, 56, 95, 128
Moibius functions, 30
Mortgage problems, 7ff

Names, mnemonic; *See* Mnemonic names

133

Output considerations, 48

Payroll problems, 6, 12, 67ff, 92
PL/I, 27, 35, 37
Prettyprinting, 17, 42, 98ff
Printout, sample, 10
PRINT statements, 37f, 123f
Problem solving, compared to programming, 125
Procedures, 16f, 86, 108f, 115
Procedure declarations, 117
Proverbs, table of, 4
Psychological set, 96

Record of control, 124
Recursion, 116ff

Side effects, 24ff
SNOBOL, 37, 50
Software quality, 125ff
Stepwise refinement, 64
String manipulation, 39f

Structure, logical, 16
Structured programming, 64
Subprograms, 15
Subroutines, 108, 111, 116
Syntactic errors, 26f
Systems analyst approach, 13, 14

Top-down approach, 11ff, 64ff
Trace, of a variable or function, 124
Traps, 124
Trees, graphical representation by, 65ff
Tricky programming, 35f, 102

Variables
   COMMON, 109, 126
   global, 25, 111, 116, 126
   initializing, 38ff
   intermediate, 29ff
   loop, 31, 34

Water jug problem, 20f